*Love That Lasts*

WHEN MARRIAGE MEETS GRACE

# *Love* THAT LASTS

GARY & BETSY RICUCCI

FOREWORD BY C. J. & CAROLYN MAHANEY

CROSSWAY BOOKS
WHEATON, ILLINOIS

*Love That Lasts*



Published by Crossway Books
a publishing ministry of Good News Publishers
1300 Crescent Street
Wheaton, Illinois 60187



Cover design: Josh Dennis

Cover photo: Josh Dennis

First printing, 2006

Printed in the United States of America



**Library of Congress Cataloging-in-Publication Data**

Ricucci, Gary.
Love that lasts : when marriage meets grace / Gary and Betsy Ricucci.
p. cm.
ISBN 13: 978-1-58134-782-1
ISBN 10: 1-58134-782-0 (tpb)
1. Marriage—Biblical teaching. 2. Marriage—Religious aspects—Christianity. I. Ricucci, Betsy. II. Title
BS680.M35R53 2006
248.8'44—dc22 2005036399

ML 16 15 14 13 12 11 10 09 08
15 14 13 12 11 10 9 8 7 6 5 4

To Betsy

*Sweetheart, I just couldn't resist this opportunity*
*to tell you once again how much I love you!*

*With each moment that we share together*
*I become more aware*
*of what a precious gift you are to me.*

***Thank you for saying, "Yes."***

# Contents

# *Foreword*

## *By C.J. and Carolyn Mahaney*

This is a difficult task. Please don't misunderstand. Writing the foreword to this book is quite the honor for us. But the task is very difficult for many reasons. Here is one such reason.

How can we introduce our dear friends Gary and Betsy to you in just a few words? How can we briefly communicate the depth and breadth of our respect for this couple whom we have known for over twenty-eight years? We could write a book about Gary and Betsy, but we've only been asked to write a foreword!

You might have already picked up on how excited we are about this book. We feel like we know a big secret that many others are about to discover. You see, we know the difference this book can make in your life because of the difference this couple has made in our lives and in the lives of so many others. And take it from us, this is the couple you want writing a book about marriage. Because Gary and Betsy are humble they didn't want to write this book, but we (and many others) felt they simply had to. In the end we persuaded them to do whatever was necessary to make this book happen. The compelling example, biblical instruction, and personal care they have provided for so long and for so many in Covenant Life Church simply had to be offered outside that local church. And here it is!

In *Love That Lasts* you will experience the effect of Gary and Betsy's example, instruction, and care. To read this book is to be personally cared for by this exceptional pastor and his godly bride. On each page you will find counsel that is biblical and wise. And you will be repeatedly encouraged by their humble example as they reveal their struggles with indwelling sin. This book you hold in your hands will transfer hope to your heart regardless of your past, regardless of your present struggle with sin, regardless of any fears you might have about the future. For throughout this book you will be reminded of the truth of the gospel, the power of the gospel to transform your marriage, and the relevance of the gospel to every area of marriage. Your marriage is about to meet grace!

So let the reading begin, and let the transformation of many marriages commence. Let couples grow and change. Let there be husbands who joyfully serve and lead, and wives who joyfully help and support. Let there be substantive communication and conflict resolution and romance and great sex, and all by the grace of God, for the glory of God!

# *Preface*

This book was first published by PDI Ministries (now Sovereign Grace Ministries) in 1992 as a very different volume, though with the same authors, nearly the same title, the same general subject matter, and the same sincere intentions.

It certainly doesn't seem like thirteen years ago that we wrote:

> With every page of this book we've had to humbly and gratefully ask ourselves, "What do you have that you did not receive?" (1 Corinthians 4:7). We didn't write this book as marriage experts, but as a couple to whom God has been very gracious. He has set us in a church where Jesus Christ and his Word are preeminent, and marriages and families are a top priority. And within Covenant Life Church he has surrounded us with friends, examples, instruction, care, accountability, and encouragement.

At that time we had been married fifteen years. In these additional thirteen years this testimony has only become deeper, richer, more of a reality, and more precious to us . . . every word of it! We say this first of all to give glory to our God and Savior, Jesus Christ, who has been so faithful to meet us time and again through his Word, his Spirit, and his church. We also share this to bring encouragement to past, present, and future readers. For every marriage, there really is hope and provision for a love that lasts!

And something else has happened in the intervening years. Many wise pastors, teachers, authors, and friends have continued to open up the Scriptures to us as they pertain to the vital topic of marriage. Then one day we realized that the set of outlines we now use when teaching on marriage has, over time, changed significantly from the set that formed the first book. So while this book covers essentially the same topics, we believe it does so in a way that sets forth more fully and faithfully the biblical view of marriage.

Anyone familiar with the original book will notice the changes, beginning with the cover. Both books share the same title, but the original subtitle, "Making a Magnificent Marriage," while certainly a worthwhile goal, seemed to put the emphasis on human effort, for human ends. The new subtitle, "When Marriage Meets Grace," reminds us that it is God and his glorious power revealed in the gospel of Jesus Christ that are the beginning, the means, and the goal of marriage. What infinite help and hope that can bring to any and every marriage!

But let's be clear, marriage is not an end in itself. God's best is a marriage that reflects the marvelous union between Christ and the church, a marriage that contributes to the Lord's purpose of building his church and preparing the next generation, and a marriage that offers hope and help to couples and families desperate for answers. We trust this book will inspire faith, provide biblical guidance, and instill in you a determination to cooperate with the ever-abundant grace of God in your marriage.

For some couples, reading this book is part of a painful search for a glimmer of hope. Others are still immersed in the rich afterglow of a recent honeymoon. But most simply want to take a next step toward a truly God-glorifying marriage. Though each situation is different, God will always honor faith, humility, and obedience—because he is faithful and his Word is true.

To those who have given so generously to make this revision a reality we want to express specific thanks. The new drafts began with Andy Farmer, a pastor in our sister church in Philadelphia, who unwittingly offered, "If there's anything I can do to get the book back in print . . ." So he took the transcripts of our updated messages and started an initial manuscript. Bo Lotinsky, with great perseverance, rode herd as manager of this project for so long, he wanted to rename the book *Love AT Last!* And the actual writing and editing process was meticulously, excellently, and graciously overseen throughout by Kevin Meath, whose many talents as a writer and advisor have made this material so creatively accessible and applicable. Your skills and encouragement were like a fine writing instrument. The ink just flowed!

To Jeff Purswell we offer our deepest gratitude for jumping in at the eleventh hour with his considerable gifts, bringing biblical, theological, and linguistic precision.

Just when we thought we might be close to finishing, my dear friend C.J. Mahaney helped us see how the book could be substantially improved. Thanks to him and his considerable discernment and editorial eye, it is now shorter, clearer, more biblical, more enjoyable, and just plain better. Thank you, C.J.—the extra effort was well worth it!

To those fellow leaders and many authors (both dead and alive) who allowed us to present or adapt their material, we say thank you, not only for your kindness and generosity but for the fruit we've seen in our own marriage as a result of your instruction.

Being aware and most appreciative of the high biblical values and publishing standards held by Crossway Books, we are more than humbled and honored by the willingness of Lane Dennis and his team to add *Love That Lasts* to their list of titles. And our thanks to Ted Griffin, Senior Editor at Crossway Books, for bringing his significant gifts and experience to this process.

Many thanks to our fellow pastors and their wives in Sovereign Grace Ministries for their constant encouragement, example, and support in this process.

And how do we thank our wonderful friends, the pastors of Covenant Life Church and their wives, and our church family at Covenant Life? Your names and faces flood our hearts with joy. You are the folks with whom we share life and family and ministry and mission. In so many ways this book happened because of you, the church home in which all of it has been shaped, developed, and shared. And in many ways this book is dedicated to you.

A specific word of gratitude, respect, and affection must go to Kenneth and Valori Maresco and Bob and Julie Kauflin, who for years have been our friends and served as leaders of our particular pastors' small group (first the Marescos and now the Kauflins). You have brought us counsel with God's wisdom, correction with God's grace, care with God's compassion, and friendship with God's love. We wouldn't be where we are today without you!

And we again want to uniquely honor our very dear longtime friends and personal heroes C.J. Mahaney—who leads Sovereign Grace Ministries and until recently served as Senior Pastor of Covenant Life Church—and his wife, Carolyn. Your wisdom, friendship, encouragement, trust, instruction, and compelling example have so informed this book and continue to profoundly influence our lives—now for more than three decades (and counting!). No one has touched our lives more than you! We can't tell you what a joy and privilege it is to continue this wonderful journey of friendship and ministry together!

Dad and Mom R., thank you for your faithful, covenant love that has lasted these fifty-nine years. And Mom M., thank you for your faithful love to Dad throughout the fifty-three years you shared together.

We would like to conclude by thanking our four children: Kelley, Courtney, Garrett, and Evan. We have held you in our arms, walked holding your hands, and enjoyed biblical fellowship with you as you have grown and matured in Christ. By God's grace you have supported us in ministry and have been forbearing with our many sins and shortcomings, while you have continued to cultivate humility, wisdom, and fruitfulness. You have filled our hearts and home with joy as precious gifts of God's grace, and we couldn't be more pleased to see each of you (and now Kelley with your husband, Josh!) taking your place in Covenant Life, our local church, where we continue to have the joy of serving the Savior together.

To each of you, and to the countless others who have touched our lives as means of God's marvelous grace, we present this book as an attempt to faithfully steward your love and kindness—all to the glory of God.

*Gary and Betsy Ricucci*

# 1

# The Journey of a Lifetime

## WHERE IT ALL BEGINS

Betsy and I sat quietly as the waiter cleared our table with polite, crisp efficiency. From our candlelit corner on the top floor of an elegant hotel, we had a beautiful view of Washington, D.C. in the summer twilight. The muffled hum of restaurant conversation was punctuated by the tinkling of silverware against china and crystal. But another sound had come to my attention. I could actually hear my heart pounding.

The date was July 24, 1977. Sixteen months earlier, I had asked Betsy out for the first time. Sixteen months of praying and desperately straining to discern if God would be so kind as to tell me, "Yes, she's the one." A few weeks earlier, Betsy's brother C.J. had noticed my mounting anxiety. Erupting into one of his inimitable fits of laughter, he chided me, "Gary, if anyone was concerned that you or Betsy might be making a mistake, don't you think somebody would have told you? What are you waiting for, bro?"

Now here we were, Betsy and I, and what a study in contrasts! She was a lovely picture of delicate serenity. And I . . . I was a mess. My heart was throbbing, my throat was dry, and the air-conditioning felt worthless. *Lord*, I cried silently, *please help me do this!*

I can't remember exactly what I said leading up to "The Moment," and that's probably just as well. I only recall that I asked Betsy if she would do me the great honor of becoming my wife. After what seemed like an eternity of silence, she said yes! That moment, and her answer, remain a matter of profound wonder to me. And for the past twenty-eight years I've lived in the joy and fulfillment of Proverbs 18:22, "He who finds a wife finds a good thing and obtains favor from the LORD."

Perhaps you have a similar memory. If so, we hope the joy of that moment still sings in your soul and that new verses to the love song of your marriage will be written every year. Many of you are probably enjoying a reasonably good marriage and anticipate finding in this book a refresher and some helpful reminders to improve your relationship. We trust the Lord to fulfill those expectations, and indeed do much more.

But perhaps the history of your marriage is tinged with sadness, or even regret. Maybe your joyful memories have simply faded with the calendar pages of years gone by. If so, please know that God can make all things new.

Yes, all things.

Most marriages begin with a sense of wonder and promise, with dreams and passion, with love and affection. Shouldn't marriage continue this way? Shouldn't passion deepen? Shouldn't love last?

We've written this book to affirm with full confidence that the answer to these questions is a resounding *YES!* But our confidence is not because we're experts (there is no such thing as a "marriage expert"). We're just an ordinary couple who have received rich instruction, example, counsel, and care in the same excellent local church for over twenty-eight years. And we're eager to share what we've learned.

As you read on, regardless of where you are right now, we want your flickering memories to be fanned into flames of anticipation and hope. We want your heart to be full of the fresh sense of adventure that led to your getting married in the first place. We want the rest of your marriage journey to be free from any baggage of passivity, resignation, unbelief, bitterness, or regret. And we want you to throw away any and all guidebooks and directions about marriage that the popular culture has provided. Because these are not based on the Word of God, they are completely unreliable: They are always changing; the dangers of the latest theory are never noted; the joy of sacrifice is excluded; and guidance to the correct and ultimate destination is nowhere to be found.

We offer this book as an alternative. We've worked hard to base what we say on the Scriptures. And we believe, because of the permanence, promises, and power of God's Word, that he will provide hope and help for every aspect of your marriage (2 Timothy 3:16-17).

This first chapter is vital because it charts the course for the entire journey, not only through the book, but through a lasting and vibrant marriage. We'll talk about a definition, purpose, and plan for marriage. We'll discuss motive, context, and assurance. And we'll spend time focusing on hope—the wonderful hope to be found in the glorious gospel of Jesus Christ. God wants you to complete this lifelong journey of marriage, and he wants you to finish well. But first you have to know where you're going, what to bring with you, and why you're making the trip.

A few years ago we took the family vacation of a lifetime, which we affectionately called "The Ricuccis' Great Wild West Adventure." It was unlike anything we could have imagined! You'll find some of the details later in the book (and someday you really ought to try it). But for the time being, here's a tip: how you plan, prepare, and participate are all critical to a successful journey—whether it's a marriage or a vacation.

Engaged couples, this book is for you too. Even if we don't address you directly, all that you read here still applies . . . or will soon. How exciting as you prepare to discover the many ways God will reveal his goodness in your marriage!

One more thing before we start . . . what a joy and privilege it is for us to join you for this portion of your marriage journey! We know you could be reading a lot of other books and spending your time in a thousand other ways, so we are quite humbled that you chose to sit down with this book. Thanks for bringing us along for the ride.

## WHAT IS MARRIAGE?

I (Gary) majored in art in college. And while my grades didn't always reflect it, I really did enjoy experimenting with the wonderful variety of composition and color, texture and tint, harmony and hue. While there are many ways art can be captured and expressed, in recent decades art has become pretty much whatever you want it to be. In 2001, for example, one of the most prestigious art awards in Europe, the Turner Prize, went to a man whose "work" was an empty exhibit hall where once in a while the lights would turn off and on! If this is art, then art can be anything, and it is therefore meaningless.

Tragically, the cultural view of marriage and family has also gradually disintegrated. No-fault divorce, prenuptial agreements, multiple pairs of parents, homosexual "marriage" . . . the definition of normal marriage and family has become distorted and confused, and the overall Western consensus that once existed on the subject is endangered.

We learn in the Scriptures that God has entrusted to the church, "a pillar and buttress of truth" (1 Timothy 3:15), the care and protection of his timeless, unchanging design for marriage. But even if many in the church at times drift into cultural confusion, we can always find the accurate definition and description of marriage in the Bible, the Word of God. In fact, the Bible is the *only* place where we can find a reliable definition and description of marriage. (If you're not a Christian, you may find that statement intolerant and narrow-minded. But please don't close this book just yet. Give us at least a chapter or two to show you the wisdom of doing marriage God's way. We think it will have been time well spent.)

What exactly, then, makes for a biblical marriage—that is, one in keeping with the Bible's teachings? Is a marriage biblical because it started in a house of worship instead of a court of law? Or because husband and wife attend church together? Or because a couple has ruled out divorce as a way to deal with problems? Or because each spouse lives a faithful and morally upstanding life? Or because it features 2.1 kids and a stay-at-home mom?

The correct answer is, "None of the above."

Those aren't even the right questions.

## THE DEFINING QUESTIONS OF BIBLICAL MARRIAGE

For the rest of this chapter we'll focus on some very different questions. Questions grounded in God's infallible Word. Questions that shed clear, biblical light on your marriage. These questions will establish the foundational perspectives we'll revisit and apply throughout this book. Every subject we discuss—roles in marriage, communication, conflict, romance, and more—will trace right back here. Most importantly, these questions can help you build a marriage that authentically honors and glorifies God by reflecting his love, his goodness, his holiness, his wisdom, his power, his peace, and his joy. From a biblical perspective, here are the defining questions of marriage.

### *Does Your Marriage Find Its Purpose Primarily in God?*

Many people, if they were totally honest, would admit that the central focus of their marriage is their personal satisfaction. In this view, marriage is a means of self-fulfillment, a path to personal happiness. I find someone who seems to complete me, who feels like my "soul-mate." My heart melts, I open myself up to her, and she to me. This view says, *I know my marriage is good because I'm happy. You complete me, and I'm so satisfied with you. Therefore, our marriage is good.*

Others say that's just selfish. *Marriage is not about me—it's about you, my spouse,* they declare. *I commit my life to making you happy. If you're happy, I'm happy. My needs aren't important. I am your noble servant, the wind beneath your wings. I exist to serve you. I must serve you!*

Still others say, *No, marriage is not about you or me. It's about us. We check our Me at the door of We. What you might need and what I might want are all consumed in the greater vision of Marriage. We live as one. We think as one. We feel as one. We are Marriage!*

The truth is, all these views have the same fatal limitation: They are centered in man rather than in God. A truly Christian marriage starts with the reality that the institution of marriage does not belong to us. It belongs to God. He designed marriage, and his purposes for it are paramount.

So then, what *are* God's purposes for marriage?

Whenever we speak of God's purposes, we must begin and end with Scripture. It is so easy to look elsewhere for guidance. We are quick to depend on our feelings, our habits, the opinions of others, secular culture, false religion, expediency, or self-will as a basis for our perspective, behavior, and decisions regarding marriage. Yet Scripture, and Scripture alone, is God's means for revealing who he is, who we are, and what marriage is intended to be.

Briefly stated, Scripture teaches that marriage is a profound and marvelous relationship—a mystery, established by God for his glory. When we speak of bringing glory to God (as we will throughout this book), we mean doing that which, to some degree, accurately reveals and represents him and appropriately honors and responds to him for who he is in his perfection and power. Thus, marriage brings glory to God by displaying as fully as possible how he relates to his people through Jesus Christ.

What is this mystery of marriage? It began in the Garden of Eden when God himself fashioned a woman perfectly suited to Adam and "brought her to the man" (Genesis 2:22). From Genesis 2:24 we glean this divine description of marriage: "Therefore a man shall leave his father and his mother and hold fast to his wife, and they shall become one flesh." So from the earliest pages of Scripture, we see that marriage—an exclusive, passionate, and permanent relationship between a man and a woman—owes its very existence to God.

As significant as marriage was in Eden, the full meaning of marriage was not disclosed until the coming of Christ. When the apostle Paul teaches about marriage in Ephesians 5, he quotes Genesis 2:24 and then draws back the curtain on this amazing truth: "This mystery is profound, and I am saying that it refers to Christ and the church." This revelation explodes all human-centered explanations for marriage. The relationship between a husband and a wife is meant to be a reflection of Christ's relationship with his church—a living parable of the supernatural union between Jesus and his Bride.

To grasp this staggering truth is both inspiring and sobering. What a privilege! What a responsibility!

For many of us, this truth reminds us not so much of God's grand design, but of how far short we fall of the divine ideal. Yet God wouldn't have made the analogy unless he intended to draw us to himself and his faithfulness for its fulfillment. It's overwhelming to realize that God intends to create and cultivate the same abundant, gracious love between a husband and wife that he has for us. In light of this glorious gift it is no wonder that Scripture reminds us that marriage is to be held in honor among all (Hebrews 13:4).

So marriage, far from being an end in itself, is a key part of God's plan to fill the earth with a demonstration of who he is. Marriage belongs to God and exists for his glory. And *that* is for our good.

### *Does Your Marriage Find Its Hope in the Gospel of Grace?*

Perhaps you noticed the subtitle to this book, "When Marriage Meets Grace." *Grace* is one of those words we hear often because it's so important . . . but then we lose all sense of how important it is because we hear it so often! Most of us could use a quick refresher course on what grace really is. Author and speaker Jerry Bridges defines grace as God's "undeserved favor to those who deserve his wrath."[1] God's grace comes to us through the gospel, and the gospel is the means by which we experience that grace. Grace redirects our focus from our guilt to God's forgiveness, from our failures to Christ's perfect righteousness, from our total inability to God's complete sufficiency, from all we feel burdened to do to all Christ has already done on our behalf.

Right now you may be thinking, *Uh, Gary, could we push the Pause button? We've talked about God, about reflections of divine reality, and now the gospel and grace. When exactly are we going to talk about marriage? You know, husband-and-wife stuff—communication, sex, children, paying the bills? So far, this just sounds like a lot of theology!*

If that, my friend, is your view, I have to tell you: Nothing is more important to your marriage than your theology (what you believe about God), and nothing is more important to your theology (and hence your marriage) than the gospel. So hang in here with me, OK?

The gospel, in brief, is the good news about the person and finished work of Jesus Christ. Consider for a moment that the eternal Son of God relinquished the glories of heaven to become a man, a human being like you and me. He lived a perfect and sinless life (unlike you and me), fulfilling every requirement of God's holy law in a way we could never hope to accomplish. And then in a glorious display of God's love for sinners like us, he willingly received the full fury of God's righteous wrath against sin by dying for our sins on a cruel Roman cross.

Because God's absolute and perfect holiness demands an equivalent holiness from all who come before him, in ourselves we are all hopelessly lost and condemned. But Jesus, who had no sin of his own to pay for, took our place, paid our penalty, and suffered our punishment. Because his death as our substitute was perfectly sufficient to pay for our sin, God vindicated him by raising him from the dead. So now all who place their trust in Jesus' work on their behalf and turn from their sin will be forgiven, counted righteous in him, and saved from judgment for all eternity . . . all by God's marvelous grace. This is the gospel. This is the good news. Better news simply does not exist!

Tragically, this most precious of all news is too often assumed ("OK, I know Jesus died for my sins"), misunderstood ("I thought the gospel was for unbelievers—I'm already a Christian"), or even ignored or dismissed ("Don't give me theology—I need help for my marriage right now"). But consider these marvelous truths.

- *Because of the gospel, Christians have become new creations* (2 Corinthians 5:17). Therefore, in our marriage, our past does not define us, confine us, or determine our future.

- *Because of the gospel, we are forgiven* (Ephesians 1:7). Therefore we can live free of all guilt and condemnation for every sin, and we can trust that God, in his mercy, will be gracious to us.

- *Because of the gospel we can forgive, just as Christ forgave us* (Ephesians 4:32). Nothing done against us compares to our sin against God. Therefore all offenses, hostility, and bitterness between Christians can be completely forgiven and removed.

- *Because of the gospel, we are accepted by God* (Romans 15:7). Therefore we are not dependent on a spouse for who we are or what we need.

- *Because of the gospel, sin's ruling power over us is broken* (Romans 6:6, 14). Therefore we can truly obey all that God calls us to do in our marriage, regardless of any circumstance or situation.

- *Because of the gospel, we have access to God through Christ* (Hebrews 4:14-16). Therefore we can at any time take any need in our marriage to the One who can do all things.

- *Because of the gospel, we have hope* (Romans 5:1-4). Therefore we can endure any marital difficulty, hardship, or suffering, with the assurance that God is working all to our greatest good (Romans 8:28).

• *Because of the gospel, Christ dwells in us by his Holy Spirit* (Galatians 3:13-14). Therefore we are confident that God is always with us and is always at work in our marriage, even when progress is imperceptible (1 Thessalonians 5:23-24).

• *Because of the gospel, we have power to fight and overcome remaining sin*, which continues to dwell and war within us (Romans 7:19-21, 24-25; Galatians 5:16-17). This indwelling enemy represents the essence of what is called *the doctrine of sin.*

These are just a few of the ways the gospel can transform a marriage. Sometimes it's not easy to live in the reality of these truths. But it is always possible—and not because of our strength or determination, but because of God's empowering and enabling grace.

If you haven't noticed, we are intent (because God is intent) on having your heart and marriage filled with the hope and grace of God's love, faithfulness, and power displayed in the gospel—the person and finished work of Jesus Christ. And God's grace is every bit as present and effective on our best days as it is on our worst. God is constant in his commitment to love, bless, and transform, not because of our performance, but because of the perfection of his Son. That is the gospel of grace. And it is grace that gives us hope.

When we grasp the depth of God's love for us revealed in the gospel, when we rest in the joy of God's forgiveness toward us in the gospel, when we experience God's transforming power in us through the gospel, and when we begin to emulate the pattern of humility and obedience we see in the gospel, what a wonderful difference this will make in our lives and marriages! Nothing is more essential to a marriage, and nothing brings more hope, than applying the gospel of Jesus Christ.

### *Does Your Marriage Find Its Home in the Local Church?*

Woefully neglected in so much of the marriage material I have come across is the vital role of the local church. Simply put, Jesus is building his church (Matthew 16:18; Ephesians 4:15-16), and the local church is the biblical home for Christian marriage, the indispensable context where love and marriage are to be lived out. Without the church we will be squeezed inexorably into the world's mold. Let's briefly examine God's provision and protection through the church.

*The church is the place where men and women exchange worldly independence for biblical humility.* As a pastor, I have often watched with great sadness the gradual erosion of a family under the influence of an independent man or woman blinded and controlled by his or her pride.

Most couples in our society have grown up breathing the cultural air of a husband's independence and a wife's feminism. Keeping our own counsel; pursuing our own goals, gratification, and fulfillment; hiding our struggles, weaknesses, and problems; being self-sufficient and self-absorbed—it's all second (sinful) nature to us. While this may make for some great executives, entertainers, athletes, and marketers, it makes for terrible marriages. We need others not only beside us but ahead of us and even over us. There is no room in Scripture for Lone Ranger spouses.

The Bible says that "God arranged the members in the body, each one of them, as he chose" (1 Corinthians 12:18). A couple who commits to a local church begins to put to death proud and dangerous independence. As they press forward, seeking to be fully known, to walk in the light, and to confess temptations, struggles, and sin, they begin to take on the raw material of true greatness—humility and servanthood. And they begin to get the help we all need but are often too proud to ask for.

Josh Harris, our Senior Pastor at Covenant Life Church, has written a fine book titled *Stop Dating the Church: Fall in Love with the Family of God.* In a wise and winsome way he provides clear biblical direction for the freelance wandering that characterizes the lives of so many Christians. He comments:

> The longer I'm a Christian, the more aware I become that I cannot live the Christian life on my own. My individual and direct relationship with God through Jesus is the greatest privilege and he is truly all I need—and yet God in his wisdom has created all of us to need others, too. Is this a contradiction? Not at all—for God has ordained that much of his grace flows to us *through* others. Says Pastor John Piper, "Sanctification is a community project."[2]

Friends, sanctification—becoming like Christ—is indeed a community project. And marriage, growing to represent Christ and the church, is every bit as much a community project.

*The church is the place where marriages are fed and supported with truth.* The local church is God's primary context for the teaching and application of God's Word. As helpful as recorded messages, Christian media, conferences, *and even books* can be, the Lord has established the church as the central depository and dispensary of truth. If you truly want to mature as a husband or wife, if you want your spouse to spiritually thrive, if you want to see your family nurtured into the truth, the local church is your God-given context.

*Finally, the church is the place where marriages are helped in seasons of need.* In every marriage there are times of trial, struggles with sin, and seasons of suffering. The loss of a job, a significant illness or injury, a financial crisis, persistent patterns of sin in one or both spouses—there are many ways in which serious trials can assault a marriage. It is at these times that our brothers and sisters in the local church embody the love of Christ to us.

One afternoon while I was in my office getting this book ready for republication, the receptionist called. A couple in the lobby was asking if they could stop in for a few moments. Down the hall I could hear a woman's familiar voice laughing and proclaiming, "Tell him not to worry. This isn't for counseling!"

It was Mike and Angela (not their real names), beaming with joy. A few months earlier I'd had the privilege of overseeing the renewal of their wedding vows on their twenty-fifth anniversary. They had come by to drop off a few thank-you gifts, ignoring my appeals that the honor of celebrating God's grace and faithfulness with them was more than enough thanks.

You see, the first time Mike and Angela had stopped by, joy was nowhere to be found. Years ago they had sat at our kitchen table, virtual strangers to Betsy and me, not knowing what to do or where to go. They only knew their marriage needed help. Thus began their journey into Covenant Life Church and many profound experiences of God's love and care expressed through his people.

Their struggles were agonizing, and their setbacks more than a few.

But God had placed them among people committed to help carry their burdens with grace and truth. Through fellow members of the Body of Christ, God met Mike and Angela at each crisis—through a sermon, a couple, a friend, a worship song, or a small-group leader ready to care, counsel, and, yes, firmly correct in love. At first, change was slow, but God was faithful, his Word true, and his church an indispensable means of grace.

I am deeply affected by Mike and Angela's humility and perseverance, and I am profoundly touched by the many dear servants who loved them at all times with fervency and faith. What can compare with the transforming power of the gospel of Jesus Christ lived out among fellow sinners saved by grace? As this precious couple sat in my office, they were radiant with the joy of forgiveness, fruitfulness, and genuine friendships. Now as I sit here recording that visit, I can only say through tears, "Lord, thank you for the cross, and thank you for the church."

Of all the leadership decisions I have made by the grace of God, the very best one has been leading my wife and family into our local church. Here we have remained for more than twenty-eight years. We were married here, our children were born and raised and are now serving here, and as I write this, one child is just weeks away from being married here! We are a part of it. It is a part of us and our entire family. For us, life, marriage, and raising children apart from the local church is literally unimaginable. Friends, this should be the norm, not the exception, for every Christian. And regardless of the cultural whirlwind around us, it is the local church—Christians living a shared life biblically before God and one another—that will ultimately secure the place and role of marriage and family from generation to generation.

## Looking Forward

So you see, the defining questions of biblical marriage posed in this chapter are more than casual inquiries. A couple's understanding of marriage must begin with God's purpose. A marriage that reflects Christ and the church must be founded, directed, and nurtured by the gospel and by grace. And a marriage can only prosper and be fruitful if it finds its home in a local church.

These are not simply a set of suggested steps to a healthy home life. Nor are they one of several possible routes to a marriage filled with God-glorifying joy. Rather, because of the authority and reliability of Scripture, we can say with confidence that they are necessary and essential to what God intends marriage (*your marriage*) to be.

The rest of this book is, in effect, an elaboration and application of the biblical truths set forth in this chapter. To do that we will take the next two chapters to discuss the roles of husband and wife. From there we will move on to the why and how of communication and the resolution of conflict. Finally, we'll end with a couple of chapters on romance and sexual intimacy. If you are eager to take the next step in enriching your marriage, or if you have encountered trials and difficulties in your marriage and are looking for help, or if your marriage has not yet begun, don't be impatient—give yourselves plenty of time to understand and apply and grow. There's enough in this book to keep you busy for the rest of your married life! So don't expect to attain perfection in the next twenty-four hours, or the next twenty-four years.

We advise you to start slowly, establish convictions from Scripture, and concentrate on becoming consistent in one or two areas at a time. Remember, the contents of this book are almost thirty years in the making, and trust me, Betsy and I still have plenty of work to do.

Too many marriages are far from what they can and should be. Even the most mature marriages are still made up of two redeemed sinners who are continually being tempted to pursue "all that is in the world—the desires of the flesh and the desires of the eyes and pride in possessions" (1 John 2:16) rather than the loving commands of God. We all have work to do. By God's grace and because of God's truth, every marriage can benefit from this book. As you read on, please don't simply scan the pages for some how-to tips and techniques. Instead, open your heart fully to the voice of God's Spirit and the work of the Savior, who can change *you* (not just what you do) in ways beyond what you can even ask or imagine (Ephesians 3:20).

Before we close this chapter, could Betsy and I offer just a couple of thoughts for your consideration? This will only take a minute.

Ladies, this is Betsy. If your husband begins to demonstrate biblical love after a long season of neglect, be patient and receive his love thankfully. Please don't think, *Oh, he's only doing that because it said to in the book. He doesn't really mean it.* It may feel that way for a while, but he needs to start somewhere. He is trying, perhaps for the first time, to love you as God intends. God's call to you is not to read this book and then judge his progress but to give yourself to God's will for you.

Guys, Gary here. The first steps to restoring or rejuvenating a drifting marriage can be very awkward. It's difficult to admit, "You know, I've never said this to you before, but in my heart I really want God's glory and your best in our marriage. I haven't done a good job at pursuing this, but I want to. I don't exactly know how yet, but please be patient with me as I try." Just this sort of simple statement is a great next step.

Whether husband or wife, it's those first steps of humility and faith, of confession and repentance that are nearly always the hardest. But note this: even *wanting* to change is an indication that God is already at work in your marriage! Already his Spirit is stirring your faith with the power of the gospel. Already he is filling your heart with hope for a love that lasts.

Friends, this is exactly what starts to happen when marriage meets grace.

2

# *Leading with Love*

## THE ROLE OF THE HUSBAND

As I (Gary) walked into a massive auditorium in Montreat, North Carolina in 1974, men of all ages were already streaming in. Among them were several elderly gentlemen with the clear-eyed look of men who had lived wise and honorable Christian lives for many decades. It was fascinating to me that, of all the seminars at the conference, they had chosen this one, on marriage. You see, along with a few other guys, I was holding down the bottom end of the age-and-experience spectrum. And though I was still single and didn't even have anyone in mind (yet), I wanted to seize any opportunity to prepare for the day when I too might say, "I do."

What happened next is etched in my mind as if it happened yesterday. We settled into our seats, and the speaker approached the podium. Scanning the audience, a wry smile crossed his face, and he began his presentation with a sentence I have never forgotten: "When you hear how much God expects of you as a husband, you're gonna want to quit."

It seemed humorous at first, and we all laughed. But the more he spoke, the more humbled, captivated, and inspired I became. I was learning that in marriage God entrusts to mere men the awesome privilege and responsibility of loving, leading, nourishing, and cherishing a woman in the same way that Christ loves his church. Amazing!

Since that day I have grown to see ever more clearly, both from

Scripture and experience, that understanding, embracing, and intentionally pursuing biblical roles are all crucial to building a marriage that glorifies God. We'll take the next two chapters to explore the critical but widely misunderstood subject of roles in marriage—from the Garden of Eden to your own bedroom.

## Starting from Square One

A big mistake many of us make in this area is to think of *role* as basically synonymous with *job description*—"just tell me what to do, so I can get on with it." We want it practical and pragmatic (am I right, guys?), as if marriage could be run from a well-structured set of his and her to-do lists.

A more modern and more serious error dismisses any significant distinction between gender roles within marriage. This view denies and often despises the whole range of biblical teaching on male and female, leadership and submission, headship and helper.

Both views are way off course. As we saw in Chapter One, if you start with man rather than God, with the creature rather than the Creator, you will never arrive at a clear, accurate view of any aspect of human nature. That's letting the world speak more loudly than the Word, and allowing personal preferences rather than biblical patterns and truth to rule our hearts.

Whenever our convictions and practices become rooted in secular culture, personal experience, pragmatism, or sinful desires—rather than in the teaching of Scripture, the inspired Word of God—confusion gradually and inevitably takes hold. How tragic that society abounds with the deeply confused and misguided people who grew up in families that went their own way (Isaiah 53:6) and did what was right in their own eyes (Deuteronomy 12:8).

In this chapter we'll see from Scripture that God created us male and female and gave us unique and distinct roles in marriage. The emphasis here will be on the role of the husband. So, men, let's take a look.

## The Origin of Roles

In the significant and much-needed book *Recovering Biblical Manhood and Womanhood* (Wayne Grudem and John Piper, general editors), John

Piper frames the fundamental biblical understanding of role differences between husbands and wives.

> When the Bible teaches that men and women fulfill different roles in relation to each other, charging man with a unique leadership role, it bases this differentiation not on temporary cultural norms but on permanent facts of creation. . . . In the Bible, differentiated roles for men and women are never traced back to the fall of man and woman into sin. Rather, the foundation of this differentiation is traced back to the way things were in Eden before sin warped our relationships. Differentiated roles were corrupted, not created, by the fall. They were created by God.[3]

Let me rephrase the main point of this quote, for emphasis. The idea of roles in marriage did not originate with *Ozzie and Harriet* or any other 1950s sitcom. It is not the archaic plan of domineering men to subjugate women. Roles are not an unfortunate by-product of God's Plan B, implemented as an emergency measure after sin entered the world. Rather, the essential nature of roles in marriage was established *before sin*.

Roles, it turns out, are a reflection of God's best, not a response to our worst! They display the wisdom of divine order and care and are designed to bring glory to God as they reflect his perfect plan for the greatest good of those he has created.

To state the case even more strongly, the concepts and roles of headship, leadership, subordination, and submission did not originate in a particular culture, period of history, or religious tradition. Defined roles and distinct functions are timeless and divine, because they are part of the order in the Godhead, the Trinity. The persons of the Godhead are one in essence and equal in nature, attributes, and perfections. They differ, however, in *role*.

*God the Father has authority over God the Son.* Jesus said, "The Son can do nothing of his own accord, but only what he sees the Father doing" (John 5:19). And, "I have come down from heaven, not to do my own will but the will of him who sent me" (John 6:38). ". . . the head of Christ is God" (1 Corinthians 11:3). And in eternity ". . . the Son himself will also be subjected to him [God]" (1 Corinthians 15:28).

*God the Son had the authority to send God the Holy Spirit.* Jesus told his disciples, "If I do not go away, the Helper will not come to you. But if I go, I will send him to you" (John 16:7). And, "He will not speak on his own authority. . . . He will glorify me, for he will take what is mine and declare it to you" (John 16:13-14).

*So headship and submission are both found in God, and one is not superior or inferior to the other.* The apostle Paul speaks of divine order, in the home and in heaven, in this same way: "But I want you to understand that the head of every man is Christ, the head of a wife is her husband, and the head of Christ is God" (1 Corinthians 11:3).

If God had no purpose or plan for creation, roles would not matter. But he does have a plan, both for creation and for redemption: to manifest who he is and how he relates to those he creates and saves. And the fulfillment of that plan requires men and women to live within the roles for which they were created.

Now that we know roles have their origin in God, let's go back to the garden to look more closely at what John Piper was talking about. Here is a passage of Scripture you may have read many times. But please read it again, slowly and carefully.

> *The LORD God took the man and put him in the garden of Eden to work it and keep it. And the LORD God commanded the man, saying, "You may surely eat of every tree of the garden, but of the tree of the knowledge of good and evil you shall not eat, for in the day that you eat of it you shall surely die."*
>
> *Then the LORD God said, "It is not good that the man should be alone; I will make him a helper fit for him." So out of the ground the LORD God formed every beast of the field and every bird of the heavens and brought them to the man to see what he would call them. And whatever the man called every living creature, that was its name. The man gave names to all livestock and to the birds of the heavens and to every beast of the field. But for Adam there was not found a helper fit for him. So the LORD God caused a deep sleep to fall upon the man, and while he slept took one of his ribs and closed up its place with flesh. And the rib that the LORD God had taken from the man he made into a woman and brought her to the man. Then the man said,*

*"This at last is bone of my bones*
*and flesh of my flesh;*
*she shall be called Woman,*
*because she was taken out of Man."*

*Therefore a man shall leave his father and his mother and hold fast to his wife, and they shall become one flesh. And the man and his wife were both naked and were not ashamed. (Genesis 2:15-25)*

The first man and woman were created equally in the image of God. They both reflected God's character, dignity, intelligence, and morality, and yet the man was given a distinct leadership role:

• in being created first from the dust of the ground (Genesis 2:7);

• in being given responsibility and authority to tend God's creation (2:15);

• in receiving the commands of God to ensure blessing (2:16-17);

• in receiving a helper to fulfill God's plan (2:18);

• in giving names to what God had created, including woman (2:20; 3:20);

• in leaving father and mother to hold fast to his wife (2:24). (Obviously Adam had no father and mother to leave, but his male descendants did.)

The woman was given a distinct subordinate and supportive (not inferior) role:

• in being created after man, not simultaneously (Genesis 2:18);

• in being created from man, not from the soil as Adam was (2:22);

• in being named by man (3:20);

• in being the suitable helper man needed to fulfill God's creation mandate to oversee and be fruitful and multiply (2:18; 1:26-28).

All of this was confirmed and reiterated in the New Testament. Paul writes: "For Adam was formed first, then Eve" (1 Timothy 2:13). "For man was not made from woman, but woman from man. Neither was man created for woman, but woman for man" (1 Corinthians 11:8-9). Paul goes on to state Adam's leadership in the fall of man: "sin came into the world through one man" (Romans 5:12-21). We see in Adam and Eve that man and woman are equal in value, yet different in their roles of subordination and leadership, following the very pattern in the Godhead (Genesis 1:27; 2:15-25).

Thus God has made man and woman to be complementary: different from each other, but with both being vital. The word *complement* means something that fills up or completes, that which fills out and makes perfect, the necessary and completing part. This complementary, God-ordained, man-woman relationship appears in its purest form in marriage.

How remarkable and revealing that secular culture recognizes the wisdom of authority, leadership, and defined roles in almost every other area of life—business, sports, entertainment, government, the military, and education—but balks at the notion that men and women should have different roles in marriage. In God's economy and wisdom, all of life and society includes roles of leadership and subordination. This is his blessing, because without it there would be utter chaos!

## Husbands, Love Your Wives

What exactly does our role as husband look like? How do we take what God did and said in the garden and apply it today? What else does Scripture teach that can guide, equip, and empower us to fulfill our call as husbands for God's glory and the good of our wives, families, and churches?

I submit to you that in one small but inexhaustible commandment we see the foundation of the husband's role and high calling in marriage: "Husbands, love your wives, as Christ loved the church and gave himself up for her" (Ephesians 5:25).

*Love Betsy as Christ loves me? Doesn't God know how selfish I can be?* Of course he does. But the glory of the gospel is that God supplies all we lack. This is probably the highest call that can be placed upon a man; yet God's grace is sufficient, and he makes us adequate.

Now for those of us who came into marriage thinking our basic functions were to earn money, mow the lawn, and supervise the remote control, this can seem overwhelming. And in a sense, it should; apart from the grace of God, it's impossible. But God is committed to our success and fruitfulness so we can reveal the riches of his grace.

The more we learn about the grace and love of God displayed in the gospel, the better we can demonstrate such grace and love to our wives. Husbands, we are called to sacrifice for the sake of our wives, and the gospel of Jesus Christ is our example and motivation. And when we sin or fall short of what we are called to, we appeal for forgiveness to a God who loved us and gave himself for us. The role of a husband doesn't begin at the altar—it begins with the atonement . . . at the cross.

Husbands, we cannot be too familiar with Ephesians 5:25-33. Memorize this passage. Meditate on it. Let us never assume we know it or are living it well enough. Let us never presume we can move on to some other teaching more significant or more central to the great call of being a husband. There is no other such teaching. This is God's call to us. Let's together read and ponder its awesome implications.

> *Husbands, love your wives, as Christ loved the church and gave himself up for her, that he might sanctify her, having cleansed her by the washing of water with the word, so that he might present the church to himself in splendor, without spot or wrinkle or any such thing, that she might be holy and without blemish. In the same way husbands should love their wives as their own bodies. He who loves his wife loves himself. For no one ever hated his own flesh, but nourishes and cherishes it, just as Christ does the church, because we are members of his body. "Therefore a man shall leave his father and mother and hold fast to his wife, and the two shall become one flesh." This mystery is profound, and I am saying that it refers to Christ and the church. However, let each one of you love his wife as himself, and let the wife see that she respects her husband. (Ephesians 5:25-33)*

As we ponder the love of Christ for us, the Holy Spirit opens our eyes to the manifold ways in which we experience God's love and hence can express love to our wives. Let's look at some of the ways in which we can love our wives as Christ loves us.

### *Love Her Graciously*

That is, not according to her performance. It is painful to think of how often my initiative, affection, encouragement, and care toward Betsy are conditional on her performance. If I'm pleased, I pursue. If I'm disappointed, I'm distant. Jesus didn't wait for the church to rid itself of every spot and wrinkle. His love encompasses the weaknesses, failures, inconsistencies, and even the sins of the church. Because his love is gracious, it is constant and active. No one on earth should experience more of my generosity, respect, kindness, sacrifice, and gratitude than my wife.

If someone asked your wife, "How do you know your husband loves you?" what would she say? Why don't you ask her? She should be able to provide a list of thoughtful, creative, and consistent expressions of your love. What can you put on her list today?

### *Love Her Sacrificially*

True love is costly. Jesus not only gave what he had—he gave himself. You may be forced to make painful sacrifices in order to uphold your marriage vows and the commands of Scripture. Loving your wife means laying down your life for her greatest good for the rest of your life.

Sacrifice means providing for her, making sure she never has to sacrifice before, or more, than you do. Each day ask yourself: *Is there some way I can give of myself to serve my wife? Where do I see selfishness in my life that hinders unreserved love for my wife? Am I withholding something of myself that would bless my wife—my attention, affection, or creativity? What is God calling me to give up because it diverts my attention and affection from my wife?*

Sacrifice means protecting her, giving particular attention to the physical, spiritual, emotional, and relational demands on her life in different seasons. I enjoy exploring used bookstores and collecting old books. How do you suppose I'd react if you set your coffee mug on my 1866 edition of J. G. Holland's *Life of Abraham Lincoln*? Exactly. And yet I can carelessly or selfishly neglect or mistreat my most priceless earthly treasure—my wife, Betsy.

Why aren't we as passionately protective when something happens to our wives as we are if something happens to our car or computer? Worse yet, why am I not grieved when I'm the one who offends her or sins against her? I want to be more protective, enthusiastic, delighted, and excited about Betsy than I am about anything else God has given me. I want to meditate on God's grace in her life and frequently remind her how important she is to me. I want to guard her jealously, whatever the cost, treating her tenderly as a priceless gift.

### *Love Her Redemptively*

I should desire to see my wife being continually transformed into an increasingly beautiful bride, just as Christ desires this for the Church. These questions can point us in that direction.

• Do I faithfully pray for her, that Jesus Christ might be glorified in her and that she might know his love and grace?

• Do I love her enough to confront and correct her sin, especially recurrent patterns of sin, and then patiently and consistently lead her into fruitful and liberating repentance?

• Do I wash her with the water of God's Word (Ephesians 5:25-27), or do I compromise her growth in godliness because my pride, selfishness, or fear keeps me from this God-given responsibility?

• Do I lead her into active involvement and service in our local church?

• Do I constantly remind her of the gospel of grace and of God's active goodness on our behalf?

### *Love Her with Understanding*

Peter pinpoints two more ways we can love our wives: "Likewise, husbands, live with your wives in an understanding way, showing honor to the woman as the weaker vessel, since they are heirs with you of the grace of life, so that your prayers may not be hindered" (1 Peter 3:7).

The New International Version translates "live with your wives in an understanding way" as "be considerate as you live with your wives." The King James Version says, "dwell with them according to knowledge." This refers to experiential knowledge, not mere information. Who is this woman you've married? What goes on inside her mind and heart? What are her fears? Her dreams?

To love your wife with this kind of understanding involves patience, perseverance, and humility. By way of example (purely hypothetical, of course), suppose you're looking over the weekly calendar together. Yes, the next seven days are pretty tight, but it looks reasonable to you.

Suddenly your wife exclaims. "How can we possibly do all this!" What do you do at that moment? Tell her she's overreacting? Tell her she's not supporting your leadership? Tell her she's in unbelief? (This is a good one if you have nothing to do for the next two or three hours.)

I recommend that you not *tell* her anything. Instead, take some time to ask questions and listen. Find out what's generating her concern. Is this plan unrealistic or too ambitious? What will be going on during the days of that week? How packed has the schedule been in recent weeks? What can you cancel or postpone? Is this her time of the month? There's probably a reason for her response, and you'd be wise to learn what it is.

Part of understanding your wife is knowing her particular temptations, weaknesses, and besetting sins. A reaction like the one I described can be evidence of things going on in her heart and life that you can help her work through. When you genuinely understand the thoughts behind your wife's words and actions, you can then graciously lead her to evaluate them biblically. This scriptural approach addresses the real need and can lead her to a place of comfort, counsel, or perhaps conviction over her sin.

Ladies, since I (Betsy) know you'll probably peek into this chapter at some point, let me offer a few thoughts about understanding. The "understanding" God requires of your husband is not an end in itself. The occasional "There, there" with a pat on the back may make us feel better temporarily, but it leaves us stuck right where we are. We should want to please God and grow in godliness. A primary means of such growth is the leadership of our husbands as they seek to love us as Christ loves the church. Also, don't make the mistake of believing that if your husband "really understood," he would certainly agree with you. We have to be not only perfectly willing to acknowledge we may be wrong but eager to have it lovingly pointed out to us when we are.

### *Love Her with Honor*

The second expression Peter mentions is honor. Some men think they're honoring their wives merely by what they don't do, such as not being harsh or reacting in anger or "doing what other men do." But honor isn't passive—it's active. We honor our wives by demonstrating our appreciation, courtesy, and respect: affirming the indications of God's active grace in their lives; complimenting them in public; commending their gifts, character, and accomplishments; declaring our appreciation for all they do. Honor not expressed is not honor. Gratitude not expressed is not gratitude.

When Scripture calls the woman "the weaker vessel," the phrase itself implies honor. Consider Paul's references to the human body in 1 Corinthians 12: "Those parts of the body that seem to be weaker are indispensable, and the parts that we think are less honorable we treat with special honor" (vv. 22-23, NIV). The implications of relating to my wife as a weaker vessel are significant. The description is meant to produce honor and respect.

I honor Betsy when I care for her more than I care for myself. "For no one ever hated his own flesh," wrote Paul, "but nourishes and cherishes it, just as Christ does the church" (Ephesians 5:29). Hate our bodies? Not exactly! We pamper ourselves with great care and attention. Our wives would be well cared for if we gave them half the attention we give ourselves.

Peter goes on to describe a cause-and-effect relationship: if we dishonor our wives, our prayers will be hindered. Mark this well. If you find particular prayer requests going unanswered, perhaps you are not honoring your wife and living with her in an understanding way. God won't let you mistreat his daughter without consequences. They may not be immediate, but they are inevitable.

## HUSBANDS, LEAD YOUR WIVES

If the *foundation* of my role as a husband is to love, then the *function* of my role is to lead. The love of a husband includes the responsibility to lead the marriage.

We read earlier that "the head of every man is Christ, the head of a wife is her husband, and the head of Christ is God" (1 Corinthians 11:3). This verse (and passages such as 1 Timothy 3:4 and 5:8, Ephesians 6:4, and Colossians 3:18-20) tells us that husbands have a God-given privilege, responsibility, and authority to lead.

### *Christ, Head of the Man*

Before you get impressed with your status as the head of your wife, note the order in which Paul made his statement. Leadership begins with embracing the fact that Christ is the head of every man. This is an acknowledgment that final authority for every detail of my life lies with the Lord Jesus Christ, my Creator, Savior, and King.

This should give our wives great comfort. If we're submitted to Jesus Christ and committed to walk humbly before him by obeying his Word and getting counsel from others, beginning with our wives, then our wives can have great confidence in our leadership.

### *Man, Head of the Woman*

As Christ is head of the man, so man is head of the woman. Yet leadership is not merely a position we are to assume—it is a service we are to provide. Your position, remember, is not one of superior worth or value. It is simply different, not better. John Piper's treatment of a husband's leadership role is outstanding. In Chapter One of *Recovering Biblical Manhood and Womanhood*, he defines masculinity this way: "At the heart of mature masculinity is a sense of benevolent responsibility to lead, provide for, and protect women in ways appropriate to a man's differing relationships."[4]

He goes on to unfold the meaning and applications of that definition. In my opinion these biblical truths could not be stated any more accurately or directly. So let's look at a few excerpts, interspersed with some comments.

> Mature masculinity expresses itself not in the demand to be served, but in the strength to serve and to sacrifice for the good of woman. Jesus said, "Let the greatest among you become as the youngest and the leader as one who serves" (Luke 22:26). Leadership is not a demanding demeanor. It is moving things forward to a goal.[5]

A biblical leader is a servant who, by God's grace and by his own example, takes others further into the will and ways of God. Do I do things *to* my wife or *for* her? Do I *direct* her or come alongside to *lead* her and serve her? A wise man leads his wife into a deeper knowledge of God and his grace, and into a deeper trust in the Savior. This frees her to truly be her husband's helper, confident that ultimately God is sovereign over all.

> Mature masculinity does not have to initiate every action, but feels the responsibility to provide a general pattern of initiative. In a family the husband does not do all the thinking and planning. His leadership is to take responsibility *in general* to initiate and carry through the spiritual and moral planning for family life. I say "in general" because "in specifics" there will be many times and many areas of daily life where the wife will do all kinds of planning and initiating. But there is a general tone and pattern of initiative that should develop which is sustained by the husband.[6]

Men, when a situation in your home requires your attention, you are to observe vigilantly, evaluate biblically, and discern prayerfully the appropriate response, then initiate the corresponding action. Whether it's the schedule, the budget, the children, entertainment, patterns of sin, serving in your local church . . . whatever the situation, we are to initiate a course of action that brings God's grace and truth to bear for the greatest good of those whom we are leading.

> Mature masculinity accepts the burden of the final say in disagreements between husband and wife, but does not presume to use it in every instance. In a good marriage decision-making is focused on the husband, but is not unilateral. He seeks input from his wife and often adopts her ideas. This is implied in the love that governs the relationship (Ephesians 5:25), in the equality of personhood implied in being created in the image of God (Genesis 1:27), and in the status of being fellow-heirs of the grace of life (1 Peter 3:7). Unilateral decision-making is not usually a mark of good leadership. It generally comes from laziness or selfishness or inconsiderate and arrogant disregard.[7]

Men, we must lead, and we must accept our responsibility to make wise and timely decisions. Decision-making is critical to good leadership. And good decision-making requires humility in seeking the counsel of

God, our wife, and others. At this point let me offer a warning, because it is at this point that many men fail. The "process" of decision-making can too often become an excuse for indolence, timidity, procrastination, and neglect. In pastoral ministry I have found two extremes in husbands' leadership styles: Some dictate, and others abdicate. In my experience, the abdicator is far more common. Ask your wife and closest friends to help you evaluate if either of these extremes describes your leadership.

One more thing about leadership—it requires faith. Biblical leadership trusts that God will guide—and if necessary redeem—whatever decision we make that is founded on a desire to honor him and love those we lead (Romans 8:28).

## DESPERATE AND DEPENDENT

Husbands, love your wives. Husbands, lead your wives. When I consider the call and the cost, I start to feel pretty desperate. Suddenly I'm far less confident in my own experience and abilities. And thirty years after attending that conference in North Carolina, the statement "When you hear how much God expects of you as a husband, you're gonna want to quit" doesn't seem quite so humorous.

But that's a good thing—a very good thing.

The desperation and inadequacy I feel when considering the fullness of the task before me (and I hope you feel the same way) is in fact the only response that can position me to succeed! *Desperate* is exactly where God wants us. Far from being a desperation devoid of hope, it is a self-despair that acknowledges absolutely no inherent adequacy, sufficiency, or competency for the task. It is a desperation that turns the eyes of faith toward the God of grace. There, and there alone, do we discover complete and perfect adequacy, sufficiency, and competence (2 Corinthians 1:20).

It comes down to this: we can love and lead our wives because, and only because, Christ first loved us (Galatians 2:20). Our role originates *in* the gospel, is empowered *by* the gospel, and is perfected *through* the gospel. We can love and lead our wives because our Savior, Jesus Christ, loved us, gave himself up for us, and leads us each day in mercy and grace.

Men, I could have easily filled this chapter with examples of my failures to love, lead, understand, and honor my wife. But that wouldn't serve you. It might make you feel better, but it definitely wouldn't serve you.

Instead, I want to draw your attention to the glorious gospel of the Son of God who cleanses us from our past and then moves us forward to a grace-filled future. Look, we have a journey to complete, and the central theme and central focus of this journey is God's perfect and unchanging love toward us, not our own failures to love our wives. So the really important question is not "How badly have I failed?" but rather, with all of God's limitless grace at our disposal, "What can I do today to trust, obey, and glorify Christ in my marriage by loving, serving, and leading my wife?"

That's biblical leadership. That's biblical love.

# 3

# *Walking in Wisdom*

## THE ROLE OF THE WIFE

"I now pronounce you husband and wife."

This statement, ladies, marks a moment of profound change. As of October 22, 1977, at about 1:00 P.M., I was no longer single but married, and no longer "Miss" but "Mrs." . . . Mrs. Gary Ricucci . . . with a new address, driver's license, and bank account. But these exciting changes were actually far less significant than the underlying spiritual reality: Gary and I had become one, an echo (however imperfect) of the relationship between Christ and the church.

With the exception of salvation, there is no more dramatic transition in life than marriage. And much like salvation, a marriage ceremony is not only a profound change but is just the beginning of a long process of becoming more completely who we have already become in essence. The person who becomes a Christian never stops learning more of what it means to live like Christ. And the woman who becomes a wife? Well, let's just say it takes far more than "I pronounce you . . ." to make us the wives God calls us to be!

What, then, does it mean to be a wife? What should our goals be? Where do we turn for guidance on these questions? All around us, a host of voices advocate a range of views. Cast a discerning glance at any form of popular culture—books, magazines, television, movies, you name it—and you'll be struck by the deep cultural confusion over what it means even to be female, much less a wife. Sadly, even segments of the church are unclear on these foundational truths.

But God isn't unclear. He created us uniquely for his glory. In his Word, the Bible, he defines husbands' and wives' roles for our greatest good. Through that same Word he gives us the wisdom by which we can fulfill those roles. God knew it would often be challenging to find our way through the tangled undergrowth of human opinion about marriage roles. How kind of him to give us the Scriptures—written guidance we can rely on as inerrant (no mistakes), authoritative (no confusion), and wise (bringing lasting fruitfulness).

## THE WAY OF WISDOM

In this chapter, while we can't possibly examine everything Scripture says about being a wife, we will look at some of the most helpful and definitive passages. We begin with a single verse—seventeen words that are remarkable in their simplicity, clarity, and scope: "The wise woman builds her house, but with her own hands the foolish one tears hers down" (Proverbs 14:1, NIV).

This verse sets forth a woman's choices in the plainest terms. We will live either wisely or foolishly. There is no third option.

How helpful, also, that this verse gives us categories for *discerning* wise living from foolish. Wisdom builds a house. *Building* is wisdom's goal, and it is the fruit of wisdom's efforts. No surprise, then, that folly has the opposite effect: active destruction.

The Hebrew verb translated "builds" in this verse can be used in a variety of contexts. When used metaphorically with reference to a household, it communicates the idea of establishing and perpetuating a family and causing a household to flourish. That is, the wise woman doesn't just build something and walk away. She builds and tends; her dedication is ongoing.

By contrast, the foolish woman's destructive and neglectful behavior tears down and overthrows her house. She pursues what appears to be best for *herself*, but does so at the expense of *her marriage*, and in the process she ultimately harms both. Tragically, because sin is deceptive, this tearing-down is often subtle, gradual, and even unintentional.

This only underscores our need to learn God's wisdom and then to attend to it with the utmost care. Paul Tripp has written, "We were never created to be our own source of wisdom. We were designed to be revelation receivers, dependent on the truths God would teach us, and applying those truths to our lives. We were created to base our interpretations, choices, and behavior on his wisdom. Living outside of this will never work."[8]

Do you want your life to "work"—to really be a life of God-glorifying fruitfulness? Then cast off your own wisdom, and adopt God's.

As a wife, mother, and homemaker, I can often reach the end of a day and think, *Now, what have I accomplished today that was really worthwhile? No brain surgeries, no deals closed, no conferences, no multi-million-dollar profits . . . Well, I scrubbed the floors, made chicken cacciatore [Gary's favorite meal], read to the children, and baby-sat for my neighbor.* But here is the biblical answer to that question: Because today's activities have furthered the building of my home, this has been a day in which, by God's grace, I have displayed true wisdom.

According to Proverbs 14:1, if the choices I make are tearing down that which is most important, then I am living as a fool. But if I am living so as to build my household, then even when I am tempted to think my efforts aren't amounting to much, I can find encouragement that I am living wisely.

## THE ATTRIBUTES OF WISDOM

Many passages of Scripture elaborate on and define more fully what wisdom looks like in a woman, and specifically a wife. In any review of such passages, however brief it may be, one must begin with Genesis 2. Here, in his own voice, God uttered the first description, the briefest description, and the most definitive description of a wife's responsibility. A single word captures both its vast scope and simple essence: *helper*.

> *Then the LORD God said, "It is not good that the man should be alone; I will make him a helper fit for him." . . . So the LORD God caused a deep sleep to fall upon the man, and while he slept took one of his ribs and closed up its*

> *place with flesh. And the rib that the* Lord *God had taken from the man he made into a woman and brought her to the man. (Genesis 2:18, 21-22)*

The New Testament goes on to paint a clear and compelling picture of how this wise wife, this helper of her husband, ought to live. One such passage appears in Paul's letter to Titus.

> *Older women likewise are to be reverent in behavior, not slanderers or slaves to much wine. They are to teach what is good, and so train the young women to* love their husbands *and children, to be self-controlled, pure, working at home, kind, and* submissive to their own husbands, *that the word of God may not be reviled. (Titus 2:3-5, emphasis added)*

Here Paul book-ends his instructions to wives with statements about how they are to relate to their husbands. Wives are to "love their husbands" and be "submissive to their own husbands."

How do I build my home and be a God-glorifying helper to my husband? Two primary ways are by loving him and by submitting to him.

We see a similar pattern in Ephesians 5, where Paul gives instructions to married couples. There he begins with "Wives, *submit* to your own husbands" (v. 22) and ends eleven verses later with "let the wife see that she *respects* her husband." Every other New Testament passage to wives takes a similar tone, directing us to "love," "submit," "respect," and "be subject to" our own husbands.

According to Scripture, then, the wife who is building her house by practicing biblical wisdom (Proverbs 14:1) can be easily identified: she's the one who is in a genuine helper relationship to her husband (Genesis 2:18), a relationship characterized by *love*, *respect*, and *submission* (Titus 2:3-5; Ephesians 5:22-24, 33b). Let's see what these three crucial attributes look like in a wife and how we can cultivate them in our own lives.

## Cultivating a Heart of Love

In the Titus 2 passage quoted above, Paul instructs wives to be, literally, "husband-lovers." The term he uses speaks of warm and tender affection. Such love calls my husband "my dearest," not "my project." Other than Jesus Christ, there should be no one I love more than Gary, and of course my husband should be the only person I love with the passion, closeness, and intimacy of marriage.

This exclusive, passionate, and tender love is part of what it means to "cleave" to one another, holding fast to one another in covenant commitment. Yet we all know that the familiarity and daily routine of marriage can gradually transform passionate devotion into something more like comfortable toleration.

How marvelous that the God who created this tender, affectionate love is also the One who enables us to express it. For the Bible gives us not only God's loving commands but also the promise that he will bless and help us in our efforts to obey him. As Carolyn Mahaney writes, "Loving our husbands—as biblically defined—is a learned response through the grace of God. The good news is that God is eager to teach us this love."[9] Indeed, as the apostle Paul told the Philippians, "It is God who works in you, both to will and to work for his good pleasure" (2:13). In other words, whatever God calls us to do, he empowers us to perform. How encouraging!

Ladies, let me recommend to you Carolyn's outstanding book, *Feminine Appeal*, quoted in the preceding paragraph. It is a biblically inspiring journey through Titus 2:3-5, God's commands to us as women, wives, and mothers. The book is rich with wisdom, humility, humor, courage, insight, care, delight, and joy and always reminds us of God's abundant grace.

So how can we appropriate that grace for devotion to our husbands? What can we do to cooperate with God in the goal of loving our husbands more and more? What steps can we take? The following, while not exhaustive, are highly effective.

### *Pray for Him and with Him*

We can begin by praying for him, bringing him before the throne of grace for God's mercy and help. A specific focus of my daily time with God is praying for Gary. What greater way to assist Gary, and what better way to cultivate increased love, than to ask for God's blessing, wisdom, grace, and mercy for him? How marvelous are these comments from Charles Spurgeon on the effectiveness of prayer:

> Prayer is the forerunner of mercy. Turn to sacred history, and you will find that scarcely ever did a great mercy come to this world unheralded by supplication. You have found this true in your own personal experience. God has given you many an unsolicited favour, but still great prayer has always been the prelude of great mercy with you. . . . Prayer is thus connected with the blessing *to show us the value of it*. If we had the blessings without asking for them, we should think them common things; but prayer makes our mercies more precious than diamonds. The things we ask for are precious, but we do not realize their preciousness until we have sought for them earnestly.[10]

No one knows your husband better than you, and no one can pray for him more effectively than you! Take up the God-given privilege of being helper to your husband in this way by making him a central focus of your prayer life.

Of course, we can also pray *with* him, hearing his thoughts and feelings and sharing his burdens. In addition to spontaneous times of prayer at home, Gary and I regularly pray when we drive together in the car. Traveling along, praying aloud together about whatever comes to mind (with the driver remaining attentive, with eyes wide open!) brings me opportunities to hear what is foremost on Gary's heart, and this often leads to rich conversation.

### *Learn to Understand Him*

The more personally I know my husband in his thoughts and feelings, the better I can serve him, and the better our marriage can be. I want to study my husband and cultivate a growing understanding of him so I can be a more effective helper to him.

When Gary comes home from the office he might, for example, be carrying concern for a needy couple. At times I can be tempted to back my emotional dump truck up to the door and unload the burdens of my day all over him as soon as he walks in. Instead, I want to grow in serving him by asking questions and listening carefully, so I can help bear his burden in an understanding way. It's not that we'll never get to the topic of my day, but I want to begin by understanding his day, by serving him.

What does he most need in that moment? A warm embrace and a

minute alone to catch his breath? Perhaps a "How was your day?" followed by more-detailed questions if I sense he is burdened in some way? Or even a gracious adjustment if it seems he is being tempted to sin through discouragement or unbelief? "The purpose in a man's heart is like deep water, but a man [or woman] of understanding will draw it out" (Proverbs 20:5). This kind of understanding takes time and ongoing effort, but that is the joy and privilege of a growing intimacy in marriage!

### *Communicate in Ways That Serve Him*

I also cultivate love for my husband when I communicate with him in ways that will serve him (Ephesians 4:29). When I'm with Gary, my tendency can be to talk about anything and everything that comes to mind, regardless of the context, simply because I love to share all of life with him. But I need to be wise, selective, and discerning in my speech.

Casual conversation, counsel, and even correction are all effective means of deepening my love for and friendship with Gary—*if* they are shared in a timely way as expressions of genuine care and commitment to his good. Sometimes he needs my encouragement, and other times my gentle admonition. Some of his ideas warrant genuine enthusiasm, others a calm expression of concern. What opportunities we have to be helpers to our husbands in these moments! Ladies, may we take to heart the words of Scripture, "Let your speech always be gracious, seasoned with salt, so that you may know how you ought to answer each person" (Colossians 4:6).

### *Demonstrate Physical Affection to Him*

A gentle touch or passionate embrace can communicate, "I want to share all of life and all of me . . . with you!"

When Gary is sitting on the couch reading, if I can I'll grab a book and sit close by. When we go to bed I'll slide over for a pre-sleep snuggle. And if we just pass by in the hallway we'll exchange a touch or quick kiss. (Actually, Gary rarely lets me "just pass by." It's usually, "Well what have we here!" And then I have to look around quickly to see if any of the kids are watching!) Just as we long for our husbands to "delight in the wife of [their] youth" (Proverbs 5:18), so we should delight in the husband of our youth. (Gary, I thought you'd like this one.) (For more on the physical aspect of marital love, see also 1 Corinthians 7:2-5, the Song of Solomon, and Chapter Eight of this book.)

### *Enjoy Shared Activities with Him*

I had little idea when I married Gary that I would know as much about military aviation as I do today. Over the course of twenty-eight years of marriage we have taken numerous trips to the National Air and Space Museum, attended military air shows at Air Force bases or naval air stations, toured nuclear-powered aircraft carriers and submarines, and stopped at locations where retired military aircraft were displayed. Initially I simply chose to demonstrate polite interest in what Gary enjoyed, but somewhere along the way—perhaps it was seeing his interest in how God has designed the physics of flight, or his appreciation and respect for the skill and courage of those who protect our country—my polite interest grew into enthusiastic participation. Delighting together has made us closer friends.

So believe me, ladies, I'm living proof—we can learn to enjoy what our husbands enjoy. Let this passage from Philippians convince you this is not only possible, it's God's will: "Do nothing from rivalry or conceit, but in humility count others more significant than yourselves. Let each of you look not only to his own interests, but also to the interests of others" (2:3-4).

To cultivate prayer, communication, understanding, physical affection, and shared activities is an act of biblical wisdom that will increase our joy and love for our husbands. And this will make for husbands, wives, and marriages that more fully radiate the glory of God.

## Embracing the Call to Respect

Respect is a second vital attribute of the biblically wise wife. Early in our marriage we may find it fairly easy to respect our husbands. We marry Sir Romance-A-Lot, convinced he is our knight in shining armor. What a wonderful man! But within a few years or months or hours, the armor begins to creak and tarnish. We begin to notice sin and weakness (usually forgetting that our own sin is also growing increasingly apparent!).

Before long, we may see even the qualities we most admire in him in a less flattering light.

If your disappointment, fear, or pride sometimes makes it difficult for you to think about or behave toward your husband with respect, don't despair. It merely proves once again you're a sinner, just like me, just like everybody else! That's no surprise to God, and because of the gospel he is fully able to help you change.

To position ourselves to receive God's grace in this area, we must begin by facing reality. The Bible doesn't mince words on this topic. Ephesians 5:33b says, "let the wife see that she respects her husband." This command is given without qualification or ambiguity. Look as long as you like. You won't find any ifs, ands, or buts in there.

But that doesn't stop us from trying to insert them, does it?

*I would respect him if only he . . .*

*But he's so . . .*

*Why does he always . . .*

*When he changes . . . then I'll respect him.*

Ladies, according to Scripture this is unacceptable. We are commanded to demonstrate respect. Let's ask ourselves some questions:

- Am I more aware of my husband's deficiencies or his strengths?
- Am I more inclined to criticize my husband (whether verbally or in my heart) or commend him?
- Have I failed to express respect for my husband because I'm so concerned about a particular area of sin in his life?
- Have I ever thought, *If I encourage him in one area, will he think I'm condoning everything else he does that's wrong?*

I suspect many wives don't appreciate just how challenging it is to lead. Throughout our marriage I've watched Gary make difficult, sacrificial, and courageous decisions for my benefit and that of our children. I regularly tell him I think he has the harder job, and I'm *glad* he does! I want him to know I'm aware of how seriously he takes his role and how grateful I am for his efforts to lead us.

Let me emphasize two words from that last sentence: *aware* and *efforts*. Both words are crucial. What am I *more* aware of—my husband's *efforts* to lead us or where he falls short in his leadership? Which would *he* say gets more of my comments?

May I never dismiss how hard he works for us by thinking, *Well, that's his job; it comes with the territory*. No. Time with the children for fellowship and training, planning vacations, fixing things around the house, making an income, accepting the responsibilities of caring for aging parents, mowing the lawn, maintaining the cars, managing the finances, you fill in the blank—all these and more are attempts to lead, direct, or provide.

Sure, I work hard too. But to be openly thankful to Gary for the burdens and responsibilities he carries is central to being his helper. It's also a joy to do it!

There is clearly a theological aspect to this as well. My respect and gratitude—or lack thereof—speak volumes about my view of God. I can only be truly grateful for the efforts of an imperfect husband if I'm truly grateful to God for the undeserved favor he extended to me in my salvation and continues to extend each day, despite *my* overwhelming imperfections. God's ongoing grace and kindness to me—when all I deserve is judgment for my sin—allow me to extend grace, gratitude, and respect to Gary. To express these things to my husband is to honor the God who is at work through my husband.

My being respectful does not mean pretending Gary is perfect. But it does mean habitually and regularly demonstrating esteem for him, in public and in private. The goal is not to boost his self-image but to affirm the role to which God has called him, to draw attention to the grace of God at work in his life, and to communicate my support of him. There are three basic avenues by which we can cultivate and express respect for our husbands: in thought, in word, and in deed.

### *Respectful Thoughts*

Develop a habit of directing your thoughts about your husband in biblical, God-glorifying directions. Dwell thankfully on his strengths rather than resentfully on his weaknesses. Thank God for the gift he is to you. Start making a written list of things about your husband and your relationship with him for which you are grateful. In so doing, you will build your house.

- What thoughts spring to my mind when I think of my husband?
- Do these thoughts honor my husband?

### *Respectful Words*

Commend and encourage your husband wherever you can. Withholding respect or encouragement from my husband has never produced good fruit. My silence or my repeated criticisms have never inspired Gary or our children. No member of my family has ever risen to greater godliness because of my lack of encouragement. We may not realize it, but when we withhold respect, what we're really thinking is, *When they're worthy, then I'll express respect.* I'm so thankful God has never treated me this way! Psalm 103:10 reminds us, "He does not deal with us according to our sins, nor repay us according to our iniquities."

- How do I speak to my husband when we are alone?
- How do I speak to him in public?
- How do I speak of him to others?

### *Respectful Deeds*

When a husband and wife are together, a wife's entire posture toward her husband says a great deal about whether she is carrying in her heart an attitude of respect for him.

- Do I show respect to my husband through my actions? How so?
- Do I freely display affection for him through appropriate physical contact (depending on the circumstances)?
- Do I listen intently when he is speaking, whether in private or in public?
- Or do my deeds communicate a lack of respect, inattentiveness, or even indifference . . . like interrupting him, looking elsewhere when he's talking, or forgetting to get to things he's asked me to do?

May I exhort you to reread and pause to consider each of the bulleted questions in the previous few pages? There may be other examples you can add to these lists. Take them all to the Savior in prayer. Discuss them with your husband. Perhaps you don't know where to begin. Maybe you're wondering, *How do I start to establish a pattern of respect and encouragement? I've done so much criticizing, my husband won't believe I'm sincere.*

Let me encourage you to take the time to sit down and think about all your husband's godly qualities. Write down what you respect, admire, and appreciate in your husband, or things you appreciate that he does for you and your family. Think also about the routine ways you benefit from your husband in regular day-to-day, week-to-week life. Consider putting some of your thoughts into a letter of love and gratitude and giving it to him to read on his own.

Once you begin finding and expressing praiseworthy things in your husband's life, you will find more and more. As George MacDonald wrote: "Obedience is the opener of eyes."[11] So look for evidence of change in your husband's life, even something small, and encourage him in that. It may well be the start of a long string of wonderful encouragements!

Do you need to repent of long-standing disrespect toward your husband? Taking these tangible steps to gain a perspective of thankfulness and appreciation for him could be just what you need to begin changing—and just what he needs to see that you mean it.

One more thing: all the godly qualities in your husband find their ultimate source in God and his grace. To recognize and affirm these things is really to be alert to God's activity and to give God praise. To fail in this is to rob God of the glory genuinely due him.

### *The Truth About Submission*

We discussed love and respect for our husbands first because, let's face it, they make submission so much easier! But I trust now we're ready to address this topic that, although widely misunderstood, is a sure cornerstone of the best and most God-glorifying marriages.

The primary biblical text in any discussion of submission in marriage is Ephesians 5:22-24:

> *Wives, submit to your own husbands, as to the Lord. For the husband is the head of the wife even as Christ is the head of the church, his body, and is himself its Savior. Now as the church submits to Christ, so also wives should submit in everything to their husbands.*

Ladies, let us begin by acknowledging the inescapable main point of this passage: submission is our divine calling, designed by God, not man! And the call to submission is hardly isolated to this text: every passage in the New Testament addressing a wife's relationship to her husband instructs her to submit.

Secular culture, of course, rejects this call, claiming instead that submission is a creation of men designed to hinder the development of women. Because submission is a supportive role (so goes the logic), it must be inferior and degrading. Not true! Genesis 1:27 informs us that man and woman are equally created in God's image; so both are needed to fully express the image of their Creator. First Peter 3:7 further communicates that husband and wife are equally "heirs of the grace of life."

If Scripture is so clear on the equal value of men and women, why do we assume that a wife's submission to her husband suggests inferiority? Because we don't understand what the concept of roles means to God.

To God, a role is never a measure of someone's value. It's an expression of divine order and wisdom. "I want you to understand that the head of every man is Christ, the head of a wife is her husband, and the head of Christ is God" (1 Corinthians 11:3). Did you know that "the head of Christ is God"? Jesus has always submitted to the Father! Jesus himself said, "Whoever does not honor the Son does not honor the Father *who sent him*. . . . I seek not my own will but the will of him *who sent me*" (John 5:23, 30, emphasis added).

The Father has authority over the Son, but it's not because the Son is inferior to the Father. Jesus is fully God, and the Father and the Son are perfectly equal. But they are in *different roles!* Roles are simply *not* a measure of superiority or inferiority. They are a means God uses to accomplish his purposes. The glorious plan of salvation unfolds for mankind *because* each member of the Trinity assumes a unique (not a superior or inferior) functional role.

And so it is in marriage: man and woman are completely equal in value and importance, but they fulfill unique roles that gloriously complement each other. One way to gain a better understanding of submission in marriage is to observe what it *shouldn't* look like. The first opportunity for a wife to submit to her husband ended in failure, and, ladies, I think there's much to be learned here.

Let's go back to the garden of Eden. The men did this in Chapter Two, but we need to take a slightly different perspective. When the serpent said to Eve, in Genesis 3:1, "Did God actually say . . .?" Eve began to doubt, question, and challenge both the goodness and the authority of God's commands. My indwelling sin—my remaining sinfulness—predisposes me to precisely the same responses.

Then, in verse 5, the serpent told her, "you will be like God." Eve immediately began to crave the "God-like" changes she thought eating the fruit would bring her. A seed of doubt from verse 1 mixed with a touch of comparison in verse 5 and Eve became dissatisfied with her status, jealous of God's authority, and quick to rebel.

Today, ladies, you and I face the exact same temptations. Placed by God in a support and helper role to Gary, my indwelling sin is quick to display jealousy, dissatisfaction, and rebellion. When my mind and heart stray from God's truth, it becomes very easy to revert to the world's view that roles are a measure of superiority and inferiority. All too easily my submission to my husband and to God—which was designed by God for my good and his glory—comes to be seen, because of my sin, as something detestable that I want only to oppose and overthrow.

That's when I need to remember that men and women are equal, just as the Father and the Son are equal. And when the Son serves the Father, he is not in the least diminished by his service. Yes, leadership and authority are obviously God-like qualities, but submission is every bit as God-like! To submit with joy to our husbands is to be like Christ, who submits joyfully to the Father. Submission follows and reflects the very pattern of the Trinity! *That*, ladies, is the biblical view of submission.

Because this view affirms the high value and complete equality of a wife with her husband, my submission to Gary does not, of course, make me a passive partner who lives only to carry out his declared will. (Yes, Jesus does "only what he sees the Father doing" [John 5:19], but remember, he lives in submission to the omniscient, omnipotent Father.) When appropriate, I will provide Gary (in humility, I hope) with my perspective, counsel, questions, and concerns. My motive is not to make sure we "do things my way," but in the hope that, by God's grace, my perspective may be helpful to Gary's leadership.

Another way I can take an actively submissive role toward Gary is through appeal—a follow-up request that he reconsider a direction or decision. From the beginning of our marriage Gary has charged me to appeal to him to get help from others should we encounter any of these situations: 1) if after repeated discussion, and no other counsel, he is making a decision I strongly believe is unwise; 2) if in my estimation there is a critical issue pending and he won't make a decision either way; or 3) if I observe unrepentant sin.

Gary has also charged me to go directly to appropriate people in our church if he is ever stubbornly unresponsive to my appeal for him to get help. How grateful I am for such wise care and leadership!

Ah yes, to assist my husband by offering my perspective, asking helpful questions, and appealing where appropriate—it sounds so simple, doesn't it? That is, until my persistent besetting sins interfere! I have made many mistakes and sinful blunders in our marriage. I have at times because of my pride (*I know I'm right, why doesn't he see it!*) or my fear (*If he decides to go ahead with this, it will be a disaster!*) expressed my opinion and asked questions in the form of angry accusations or demands. I have also at times withheld sharing my perspective with Gary because I felt my sin disqualified me from having anything helpful to say. Far from being helpful and submissive, both extremes are actually selfish and destructive.

As Carolyn Mahaney has written, "God has graced each of us with unique gifts that he intends for us to use to support our husbands. We are to contribute our ideas and suggestions, offer wisdom and insight, pray and encourage, as well as correct. When we carry out these acts of service in all humility, we help our husbands to lead, and fulfill our biblical duty to submit."[12]

When I offer counsel to Gary, ask him questions, or make an appeal, these are key expressions of my God-given role as his helper, and as such they are a deep honor. It gives me joy to do these things for Gary because it places me squarely in the middle of God's good and perfect will for my life. What a privilege to participate in making the one I love most on earth a successful leader!

As much as I do love serving my husband, when all is said and done, I can only live in biblical submission toward Gary because I have faith in God and his design for marriage, a faith that trusts God to lead my husband in leading me. The same good and loving God who designed the wisdom of the cross also designed the particulars of my role as a wife, including submission. And he did both of these things for his glory and my greatest good. I trust God in his design for salvation *and* in his design for my marriage. My ultimate confidence is not that Gary is all-wise, all-knowing, and all-powerful, but that God is!

## PROVERBS 31 AND YOU

John Piper succinctly defines "biblical submission for the wife [as] the divine calling to honor and affirm her husband's leadership and help carry it through *according to her gifts*" (emphasis added).[13] This matter of a wife's specific gifts ties in, of course, to what we were just discussing about giving counsel, asking questions, and making an appeal. It's also the perfect opportunity to take a look at that multi-talented woman depicted in Proverbs 31:10-31.

**Proverbs 31:10-31**

*10An excellent wife who can find?*
*She is far more precious than jewels.*
*11The heart of her husband trusts in her,*
*and he will have no lack of gain.*
*12She does him good, and not harm,*
*all the days of her life.*
*13She seeks wool and flax,*
*and works with willing hands.*
*14She is like the ships of the merchant;*
*she brings her food from afar.*
*15She rises while it is yet night*
*and provides food for her household*
*and portions for her maidens.*
*16She considers a field and buys it;*
*with the fruit of her hands she plants a vineyard.*
*17She dresses herself with strength*
*and makes her arms strong.*
*18She perceives that her merchandise is profitable.*
*Her lamp does not go out at night.*

*19She puts her hands to the distaff,*
*and her hands hold the spindle.*
*20She opens her hand to the poor*
*and reaches out her hands to the needy.*
*21She is not afraid of snow for her household,*
*for all her household are clothed in scarlet.*
*22She makes bed coverings for herself;*
*her clothing is fine linen and purple.*
*23Her husband is known in the gates*
*when he sits among the elders of the land.*
*24She makes linen garments and sells them;*
*she delivers sashes to the merchant.*
*25Strength and dignity are her clothing,*
*and she laughs at the time to come.*
*26She opens her mouth with wisdom,*
*and the teaching of kindness is on her tongue.*
*27She looks well to the ways of her household*
*and does not eat the bread of idleness.*
*28Her children rise up and call her blessed;*
*her husband also, and he praises her:*
*29"Many women have done excellently,*
*but you surpass them all."*
*30Charm is deceitful, and beauty is vain,*
*but a woman who fears the Lord is to be praised.*
*31Give her of the fruit of her hands,*
*and let her works praise her in the gates.*

Can you do all the wonderful things for your family described in those verses? I certainly can't! That's why I'm thankful this passage is not included in the Bible to taunt us with how far short we come as godly wives. Instead, it is meant to inspire us with the breadth and scope of a wife's gifts. This section of Scripture is actually an acrostic, with each verse beginning with a different letter of the Hebrew alphabet. In a sermon on this passage, John Piper comments:

> Why do people write acrostics? Because there is something in us that loves to praise what we enjoy. We like to pile up the praiseworthy attributes of people we love. Well, that is what is happening in Proverbs 31. Verses 10-31 are an acrostic. Every verse begins with a different letter of the Hebrew alphabet. . . . This is helpful to know because it tips us off that the author is not building an argument like Paul does in Romans. Instead he is stringing pearls. He has set himself the task, as he says in verse 30, to praise the woman who fears the Lord. To do this he tries to think of 22 praiseworthy things to say about her.[14]

I received a letter from a friend sharing her response as she looked at Proverbs 31 this way. This is what she wrote:

> Understanding Proverbs 31 as a string of acrostic pearls helped me dream a hopeful dream of becoming a woman whose traits will be an adorning work for my husband and children, and no longer a "boy, do I fail on multiple accounts" list. It has helped me realize this portion of Scripture was constructed with praise in mind, and that I, too, can think of what is praiseworthy in this section of Scripture and be inspired, knowing that even if I don't sew, or buy my food from merchant ships, or dress in fine linen, I can find a good bargain on clothes for my family at the outlets, and fear the Lord, and seek to do what is praiseworthy before the Lord. If I posture myself to work on the beauty within, to fear the Lord, and rise to the example of this Proverbs 31 woman, at the very least I know I have sought to be God's girl and not a product of *Woman's Day* or *Cosmopolitan*. No longer is Proverbs 31 a list of impossible dreams, but instead it is now poetry, created to inspire me to be more than I am.

Amen! I trust that we, like my friend Carol, will never look at Proverbs 31:10-31 the same way again.

Here are two more of my favorite quotes on these verses, both from Derek Kidner. He speaks of the capable wife as one "whose influence spreads far beyond her home, though it is centred there and though her achievements are (as she would wish) valued most of all for their contribution to her husband's fortune and good standing."[15]

He later notes, speaking of this passage of Scripture, "It shows the fullest flowering of domesticity, which is revealed as no petty and restricted sphere, and its mistress as no cipher. Here is scope for formidable powers and great achievements—the latter partly in the realm of the housewife's own nurture and produce (31); and partly in her unseen contribution to her husband's good name (23)."[16]

In other words, God has given women a tremendous capacity for worthwhile accomplishment, and he calls us to use it in service to others, according to our gifts. The first person I should be serving with my gifts is my husband. Consider, in light of these words of Jesus, the wife who biblically serves her husband: "The greatest among you shall be your servant" (Matthew 23:11).

Our Lord's statement has more significance than you may realize. Imagine a king and his chief advisor. One has the position of leadership; one has a position of influence. The advisor is obviously the king's servant; yet history shows time and again what an immense impact a trusted counselor can make. It's much the same within marriage. While the husband holds the position of leadership, his wife retains a tremendous position of influence.

Scripture gives us two vivid and powerful examples of the influence of a wife—one for great good and one for great evil. Through a courageous and respectful appeal to King Ahasuerus, Queen Esther was able to deter him from annihilating all the Jews throughout the Persian Empire (Esther 8). On the other hand, Jezebel treacherously murdered an innocent man in Ahab's name simply to get his vineyard and convinced the king to worship false gods. First Kings 21:25 records, "There was none who sold himself to do what was evil in the sight of the LORD like Ahab, whom Jezebel his wife incited." Ladies, be encouraged, be humbled, and be sobered. We have influence.

While worldliness grabs for the visibility of a leadership position, godliness serves, often unrecognized, in a position of influence. And as Scripture testifies, that godly influence can certainly have eternal significance: "Likewise, wives, be subject to your own husbands, so that even if some do not obey the word, they may be won without a word by the conduct of their wives—when they see your respectful and pure conduct" (1 Peter 3:1-2).

My role toward Gary is not that of a critic, passing judgment on whether he is leading effectively, properly, or correctly. Nor am I to be merely a passive recipient of his leadership. I am to be an active participant in making his leadership both effective and successful. I have a stake in this! My help is crucial to the success of my husband's leadership. How kind of God to design marriage this way!

Sometimes, as Gary's helper, my assistance to him takes a very practical form. For example, although Gary definitely leads us financially, I help him by keeping the books. And when both our sons were being homeschooled, I would adjust their school schedules so Gary's desire to meet with them weekly would work out. What a joy to contribute to his leadership of our boys and to bless in any way the growing relationships between the men in my family!

There are also a number of smaller household tasks I easily attend to. Now, Gary is very careful about what's appropriate for me, but hey! . . . I can get out the paintbrush and touch up the nicked corners. And on a warm summer day when the menfolk are all attending to other tasks, I thoroughly enjoy cutting the grass . . . getting some exercise and taking in the sun.

## The Excellent, Imperfect Wife

I want to close this chapter, ladies, with a verse I love, both for what it says and for what it does not say: "An excellent wife is the crown of her husband" (Proverbs 12:4a). I'm so glad it doesn't say, "a perfect wife" because I know I'm never going to get there! But even though perfection will always elude me in this life, excellence is definitely something I can pursue!

What is this excellence God speaks of? Remember, it's not a single, objective standard that only a few Proverbs 31 superwomen can attain. An excellent wife is a woman endeavoring by God's grace to give her utmost to the great call of being a faithful and godly wife—and God gives grace where he intends to reveal grace. It's about serving in humility, with a focus on God's glory, according to our gifts. It's about being committed to serving and growing and changing in these areas and being a helper to our husbands, not about having attained some particular level.

A wife of six months may be an excellent wife, and a wife of sixty years too—but the way excellence looks in their marriages will be very different. There are all kinds of excellent wives, and no two of them need be exactly alike!

Referring to Proverbs 12:4a, Charles Bridges comments that the excellent wife "is not the ring on her husband's finger, or the chain of gold around his neck. That were far too low. She is his *crown*, his brightest ornament; drawing the eyes of all upon him, as eminently honoured and blessed."[17]

This is the way of wisdom for me and for you. The wife who lives with biblical wisdom toward her husband will, by the enabling grace of God, exhibit love, respect, and submission toward her husband and will serve him according to her gifts. No matter how long you have been married, to be a wise, godly wife is to embrace a great call and to become a great crown.

Ladies, this is the only chapter of this book written exclusively to us. And while this book contains important truths for both husbands and wives, let me encourage you to reread this chapter, mark it up, take notes, and return here frequently. We trust that in these pages you will find much help and hope for doing all you can, by God's grace, to cooperate with your husband in creating a love that lasts.

Won't you join me in this lifelong pursuit and practice of true and lasting wisdom? I can't wait to see what God will build!

4

# Relational Intimacy

## THE GOAL OF OUR COMMUNICATION

Maybe you've experienced something similar . . . Betsy and I had spent the evening with friends in our home and were cleaning up the kitchen before going to bed. Had you watched us working together, you would have thought we were the model of marital harmony. But then I realized I could still catch the sports on the ten o'clock news. Sensing a convenient pause in our conversation, I slipped downstairs, rationalizing that most of the work was done anyway. And our conversation? Well . . .

When I came back upstairs, the house was clean. Everything was put away, and the kitchen was once again spotless. And Betsy was quiet . . . really quiet. At first I thought, *Well, she's had a long day. She's probably tired. Maybe she doesn't have much to talk about.* (Sure, Gary!) But as she continued her bedtime preparations in silence, it began to dawn on me: *Hmmm, it feels a bit "cool" in here.*

At times like these it's easy for husbands to assume (or perhaps simply to pretend) that all is well. If there's no open conflict, there's no problem, right? How quickly we slide into that passive, selfish, deluded condition that believes no news is good news. How easily we forget that the goal of marriage, and the purpose of communication in marriage, is so much higher and better than merely getting along. God made husbands and wives for all-encompassing relational intimacy.

## Created to Be Close

When God created the heavens and the earth, he repeatedly evaluated every aspect of his work as "good." In fact, the only thing in all creation that God identified as a problem at that time was Adam's solitude. When God saw that Adam lacked a suitable companion, he said, "It is not good that the man should be alone" (Genesis 2:18). How striking that the first "not good" of creation was about human isolation.

To solve Adam's problem, God created Eve. He certainly could have scooped up a fresh handful of dust and made her, like Adam, from scratch—a totally independent creature. But he didn't. In a powerful statement of the interdependence of marriage, God chose to form Eve from one of Adam's ribs (Genesis 2:18-23). She was, as Adam said, "taken out of Man."

Please remember: this is not fiction or fable. The Creator made the first wife from a part of her own husband. God's point could not be more clear. Married men and women—equal before God in dignity and value but different in function and role—have an inherent, God-given call and desire to regularly fit back into one another's lives, living in intimate companionship and fellowship with one another.

God's initial observation ("It is not good that the man should be alone") was not one that Adam had come to on his own. God had to tell Adam, just as he needs regularly to remind us. Even in the union of marriage, husband and wife can be tempted to pull back from each other and live in a measure of isolation, even when sitting together on the same couch. We become distracted by other things and drift from one another and the relational intimacy God intends for marriage.

Occasionally in these chapters we'll be using *communication* and *fellowship* somewhat interchangeably. Sad to say, but these words are terribly underappreciated. For our purposes, they both refer to something so much more than casual conversation or superficial social interaction. Drawing from its uses in the New Testament, fellowship takes place when Christians relate with one another humbly and honestly in specific, personal ways about our shared life in God. J. I. Packer writes:

> Christian fellowship is an expression of both love and humility. It springs from a desire to bring benefit to others, coupled with a sense of personal weakness and need. It has a double motive—the wish to help, and to be helped; to edify, and to be edified. It has a double aim—to do, and to receive, good. It is a corporate seeking by Christian people to know God better through sharing with each other what, individually, they have learned of him already.[18]

As it applies to marriage, we can define fellowship as *sharing all of life so as to reflect our union with Christ and deepen our relational intimacy with one another so as to glorify God and grow in godliness*. Isn't that what you really want in your marriage? Isn't it good to know that, from the beginning, this has been God's intention for every marriage, including yours?

## PURSUING RELATIONAL INTIMACY

Before Adam and Eve sinned, they were naked, yet unashamed (Genesis 2:25). Having nothing to hide, they were completely open and intimate with one another; their relational intimacy was totally unhindered. But as soon as they sinned by eating the forbidden fruit, that changed, and they recognized it. "Then the eyes of both were opened, and they knew that they were naked. And they sewed fig leaves together and made themselves loincloths" (Genesis 3:7).

Thus, when sin entered the world, its immediate effects were fear, self-focus, and shame. That leafy wardrobe represented much more than a sudden concern for modesty. Adam and Eve were acutely self-conscious, fearful, and proud. So their immediate impulse was to hide—not just from God, but from each other. It's the same for you and me today. Our sin will tempt us to hide, withhold, withdraw, and avoid. And yet God calls us as his disciples to walk in the light with him so we can have fellowship with one another in him (1 John 1:7). Indeed, *a husband and wife can only thrive in relational intimacy when they open themselves up to one another by the means of fellowship and biblical communication.*

### *Relational Intimacy Requires Honesty*

This means, in part, being completely open in our communication. My spouse should never doubt my sincerity or willingness to disclose myself. If a husband won't let his wife into his life, her ability to be his helper is severely limited. I must share my thoughts and feelings, my struggles and fears, my successes and joys, my failures and sin. If I don't, I'm not being *quiet*—I'm being proud and dishonest (see Proverbs 18:1; 28:13)! If the wife doesn't open up to her husband, he will lack the input he needs to serve and lead her effectively. In either case, the fellowship and growth meant to occur in this unique relationship will succumb to the numbing impact of selfish, secluded independence and pride. The extent to which we are completely honest about our temptations, struggles, failures, and sin is the extent to which we will experience humble communication, biblical truth, and God's transforming grace.

A word of caution: open and honest communication has nothing to do with the secular popularity of "saying what you feel," a noble-sounding sentiment that often serves as an excuse for spouting whatever is on your mind. In the Bible, the one who freely and habitually speaks his mind is neither noble nor admirable. He's a self-centered fool (Proverbs 29:20).

### *Relational Intimacy Requires Humility*

One of the greatest hindrances to fellowship in a marriage is pride—self-confident, self-exalting, self-protecting pride. Pride is perhaps the most deceptive, pervasive, and multifaceted form of sin, and it plays a central role in virtually all sin. One way the foolishness of pride is displayed in our communication is in our love for our own voice and opinions. Consider this proverb, just one of many that ties our speech to wisdom and foolishness: "A fool takes no pleasure in understanding, but only in expressing his opinion" (Proverbs 18:2).

- Pride loves to talk, reveling in every self-exalting form of self-expression.
- Pride is quite content with what it already knows.
- Pride assumes I already understand everything I need to.
- Pride assumes I don't need help.

• Pride sinfully judges others by assuming they will respond negatively or unhelpfully if I am open.

• Pride uses conversation as broadcast time.

• Pride doesn't need a spouse, just an audience.

• Pride denies what the gospel reveals about our seriously sinful condition (Proverbs 10:19; Galatians 5:17).

Whenever Betsy poses a question or concern about my tone of voice, manner of speech, or choice of words, and my first response is to "explain" or "defend" rather than ask a lot of questions about what she heard, invariably I am confirming her concern and am guilty of pride.

In contrast, humility yearns to learn, because it recognizes its deficiencies (Proverbs 12:15).

• Humility asks questions and loves dialogue.

• Humility has never found someone it couldn't learn something from.

• Humility assumes there is always more to learn about everything.

• Humility assumes I need others.

• Humility would rather be open and vulnerable than closed and independent.

• Humility uses conversation with a spouse to explore new worlds.

• Humility puts energy and effort into listening.

• Humility treats a spouse as a fellow traveler on the road to biblical wisdom.

• Humility that leads to intimacy takes an interest in one's spouse as a gift from God.

• Humility believes what the gospel says about our desperate need for God and his grace—*after* we're saved as well as before.

C. J. Mahaney has written an excellent book called *Humility: True Greatness*. I can't recommend it highly enough. In it he defines humility as "honestly assessing ourselves in light of God's holiness and our sinfulness." How do you assess yourself? Understanding and applying a clear definition of humility becomes all the more critical when we consider that God resists the proud but gives grace to the humble (James 4:6; 1 Peter 5:5).

*Humility and listening closely.* A primary way humility is expressed in biblical communication is in listening to our spouse. Most of us think we listen much better than we do. We often equate listening simply with not talking. But if most of our listening is spent formulating our next opinion or running through tomorrow's to-do list, we aren't listening at all. I (Gary) tend to think of this as efficient multi-tasking. Selfish disrespect and pride would be a more accurate assessment.

By contrast, true listening is an active, attentive commitment to understand another person and to discern relevant truth from what he or she is saying. When Jesus said, "He who has ears to hear, let him hear" (Matthew 11:15), there was a clear implication that not everyone within the sound of his voice was truly listening or hearing.

The way you listen to your spouse profoundly affects your communication. Good listening and attentiveness means undivided attention: turning off the radio, tuning out other conversations, or putting down the newspaper with a view to learn and serve. If you're at a restaurant, it means making sure you end up sitting where you won't be distracted by other people—or by the thirty TV screens. (What are you doing in that restaurant when you're out with your wife anyway!) Maintain good eye contact when listening to your spouse. Look at one another! If that's awkward, make the awkwardness the topic of conversation. Attentive listening and intentional responsiveness are expressions of humility and respect.

*Humility and asking questions gently.* Even after twenty-eight years of marriage, there are still plenty of times when I don't understand what Betsy is feeling or thinking. That's okay. Neither of us expects the other to be a mind reader (most of the time). What's crucial, though, is that I show Betsy my desire to understand her by listening and asking careful questions.

Let's say Betsy tells me she doesn't think she's being a good wife. And let's say (again hypothetically) my response is, "Come on, dear, that's ridiculous! Of course you're a good wife. Would you please pass the salad?" Now, will she just sit back, breathe a sigh of relief, and thank me for my heartfelt assurance? I don't think so.

Or perhaps in that instance I do ask some questions. That's an improvement, right? Well, maybe not. It depends on my goal. Am I interrogating her just to try to prove she's wrong? This adversarial approach simply exposes my arrogant assumption that there is nothing truly important I can learn from Betsy about what's really going on. Or, do I intend merely to sift through her answers for enough facts to "fix" her problem? In either case I've still totally missed the mark: to pursue relational intimacy with my wife, that I might know her, love her, and more effectively serve her.

So instead of flippantly dismissing her concern, grilling her like a prosecutor, or mechanically exercising my data-analysis skills, let's imagine I'm a little more humble and Christlike in my leadership. If so, I'd recognize this as a time for listening and attending to my wife's heart. I'd realize I must try to pose wise, gentle questions to find out why she feels that way, what has triggered her comment, and what she sees in our marriage that causes her such a concern.

Asking good questions with gentleness is an essential part of listening that is humble, actively involved, and intent on furthering unity. Such questions (crafted to elicit more than a yes or no) will draw out of your spouse what's really going on in his or her heart and mind. The goal is to help make sense of underlying attitudes and emotions by exposing them to the light of God's grace and truth. As Paul Tripp has written, "Gentle talk . . . comes from the person who is speaking not because of what he wants *from* you but what he wants *for* you."[19]

## Pursuing Holiness through Relational Intimacy

The relational intimacy we have been discussing is, in essence, a spiritual intimacy. As you employ biblical communication to open up to one another in all honesty and humility, you and your spouse move toward the unhindered relational intimacy that Adam and Eve enjoyed prior to their sin. As you grow spiritually closer to one another, you position yourselves to experience God's grace to help you grow in holiness, a process called sanctification. God changes you. This makes you more like Christ as individuals and makes you as a couple into a better representation of Christ and the church.

Thus, the biblical communication that furthers relational intimacy *in* marriage promotes God's ultimate purpose *for* marriage. Relational intimacy is not only enjoyable in itself—it is a path to holiness, and that brings glory to God.

### A Commitment to Grow and Change

In his Sermon on the Mount, Jesus articulated one of the most significant truths about communication in the Bible. "The good person out of the good treasure of his heart produces good, and the evil person out of his evil treasure produces evil, for out of the abundance of the heart his mouth speaks" (Luke 6:45).

Simply put, what we say (or all too often don't say) reflects the content of our hearts—inevitably, necessarily, and inescapably. We'll deal with the negative implications of this verse when we discuss conflict, but for now let's examine the wonderful potential this truth reveals for our marriages.

Once we become Christians, and the truth of the gospel takes root in our hearts, it bears good fruit. As our rebellion, bitterness, selfishness, and pride begin to be addressed by the Spirit of God, we begin to change, gradually becoming more like Christ.

While God is always faithful to lead us along the path of sanctification, the process does not happen automatically. We must cooperate with the work of the Spirit in our hearts through obedience and application of the Scriptures. The Puritan writer John Owen noted that God's Spirit "works *in us* and *through us*, not *against us* or *without us*."[20] Paul tells us in Galatians 5:16-25 that if we walk by the Spirit as we are led by the Spirit, we will experience the fruit of the Spirit—the character of Christ being formed in us. He also tells us, in Ephesians 4:11-16, that speaking the truth in love is directly tied to increased spiritual maturity (by "truth" Paul means the gospel and sound doctrine). And as we become more like Christ, it will be reflected in our speech, just as Jesus said.

### The Habit of Spiritual Discourse

There is definitely an important place in marriage for casual conversation. However, to be practicing biblical communication fully, the overall diet of conversation between husband and wife must be intentional—it must be done with a view toward bringing glory to God by becoming more like his Son.

One sad reality of married life is the tendency to move spiritual conversation to the bottom of the communication agenda. Many Christian couples, thinking back to their courtship and early days of marriage, can recall hours spent talking about God and his work in their lives. Yet over the years this type of intimate fellowship often fades away like the memory of a pleasant dream. Why is that?

Certainly one threat is the dulling effect of busyness and routine in marriage. We can end up, in effect, worshiping efficiency and productivity at the expense of regular conversation about God, his Word, and his ways.

Worldliness is another enemy. We tend to talk about what is uppermost in our hearts and minds. Have you ever tried to have a meaningful conversation with your spouse about spiritual matters, only to find each sentence painfully labored and lacking in passion? But then, when the subject shifts to a movie you recently saw together, suddenly the conversation comes alive! An energetic, nuanced, and insightful dialogue emerges naturally, covering plot, acting, editing, and the intricacies of the film. Hmmm . . . So are our minds and affections set on things above or on things on the earth (Colossians 3:1-3)? Based on your conversations with your spouse this week, what would you say you are most passionate about?

Paul recognized the vital relationship between our passions and what we talk about. For our conversations to be spiritually nourishing, our hearts need to be full of God's truth. To the Colossians Paul wrote this exhortation:

> *Let the word of Christ dwell in you richly, teaching and admonishing one another in all wisdom, singing psalms and hymns and spiritual songs, with thankfulness in your hearts to God. And whatever you do, in word or deed, do everything in the name of the Lord Jesus, giving thanks to God the Father through him. (Colossians 3:16-17)*

There's no secret to spiritual conversation. It will flow from hearts set upon God's Word. Like all good fruit, edifying conversation comes from seed sown and cultivated over time. We must *let* the Word of God dwell richly in us.

Have you let the Word dwell in you richly? In your marriage, consistently? If not, how will you cultivate fresh passion for Jesus Christ, his church, and the lost? How will you deepen your hunger and thirst for righteousness? How will you ignite your zeal to inspire the fresh pursuit of God and godliness in your marriage?

As one who has "been there, done that" more often than I care to admit (yes, Gary again!), let me suggest that we begin by talking not *about* God, but *to* God. We must confess as sin our idolatrous love for other things. We must repent of having more passion for the good things God gives us than for the God who gives all good things. In all humility and sincerity we can then ask God to change us from one degree of glory to another (2 Corinthians 3:18). Finally, we must take the time to think very concretely about what those changes would look like and what we can do to cooperate with God in getting there.

As we plant the seed of the Word through devotional reading, study, and listening to the preached Word in church, God's truth will find its way more and more into our thinking, and hence into our communication with our wives.

Guys, our wives would love nothing more than to have us share what we are learning in our reading, study, and times of fellowship with God. They want us to teach them (not preach to them) and to converse with wisdom from God's Word. This leads us to some crucial questions:

- Are you regularly reading the Bible and books that help you know and love God?
- Are you growing in your knowledge of God and his Word?
- Do you have a plan for regular reading and study?

I can't count the number of times, during the past twenty-eight-plus years of pastoral ministry, that an individual or couple has come to me with a persistent problem or struggle with sin notably *present*, yet the consistent practice of fellowship with God notably *absent*. And so often when I raise with a husband his relationship with God, he wants to focus on his relationship with his wife. Men, there will be no progress in leading and loving your wife if you fail to fellowship with God.

In my experience, healthy and growing marriages are invariably led by men who are consistent and intentional in their pursuit of God. Struggling marriages usually are not. It's just that simple.

Once you've begun a practice of seeking God and studying his Word, talking about him with your spouse will come quite naturally. Perhaps the conversation can begin with the same invitation extended by the psalmist: "Oh, magnify the LORD with me, and let us exalt his name together!" (Psalm 34:3). From there we can extol the awesomeness of the God who has saved us . . .his riches we are experiencing in the gospel . . . the great truths of redemption . . . the wonderful evidences of his activity in our lives . . . the privileges of being his children . . . The topics are limitless! It becomes an overflow of the heart, not catchphrases we master. OK, we don't have to sing psalms to each other while sitting in a coffee shop, but true spiritual discourse will produce worship in our hearts that will inevitably find some form of outward expression.

## THE PROMISE AND THE HOPE

Marriage stands apart from all other human relationships. What makes it unique is the promise of relational intimacy that God has designed into the fabric of marriage. No other relationship—with children, siblings, parents, or friends—is meant to produce the intimacy that characterizes marriage. But this oneness is not the elusive Gold Medal of Marriage—desired by all, but granted only to the exceptionally gifted and diligent. Rather, it is assumed in the Scriptures that every couple has access to this remarkable, supernatural level of ongoing unity because of our union with Christ. In fact, the absence of a growing intimacy between husband and wife, although tragically accepted in many marriages as "just the way things are," is in fact evidence of a series of choices to deviate from God's will and his abundantly available grace.

But before you look at your marriage union and perhaps begin to labor under the weight of discouragement, remember the gospel and grace. Remember that God is at work in your marriage for good. His love and power are far more effective than your weakness, failure, and sin. Remember also that in your marriage, as in your life, sanctification is both a gradual and a continual process. You are in a process of becoming less like the world and more like Christ. No matter where your marriage is at this time, it can get better. And by God's grace, it will!

Don't think for a moment that the best communication and the deepest relational intimacy between you and your spouse happened before your wedding. (I still remember one phone conversation I had with Betsy that took so long, a friend of my parents actually drove to our house to talk with them because he couldn't get through on the phone!) Was your engagement full of fresh excitement and promise? Remember how you couldn't wait to hear one another's voice? Was learning about each other a continual thrill? Great! But don't imagine it can't get far better, deeper, closer, and more satisfying. The authority of Scripture and our twenty-eight years of experience say it can!

Marriage is *not* about a deliriously happy couple getting to the altar in a flush of excitement . . . and then spending fifty years merely relishing the memories of an intoxicating engagement. One of the great joys of marriage is realizing that the wedding isn't nearly the ultimate in closeness. It's only the beginning!

God created us to communicate, and the real adventure of relational intimacy simply awaits our ongoing cooperation with the grace of God. When we pursue communication and fellowship with humility and honesty and spiritual discourse, there is no limit to the breadth and depth of relational intimacy we can enjoy!

Beginning that journey of joy is only a conversation away.

# 5

# *Grace to Those Who Hear*

## THE CONTENT OF OUR COMMUNICATION

Betsy and I are an endangered species. We are among those nearly extinct telephone-and-paper people, swept along in a digital world of e-mail, memory sticks, and PDAs. Whatever happened to leisurely conversations, elegant stationery, and fine writing instruments? I'll tell you what happened. Technology happened.

Modern technology has revolutionized everything, especially how we communicate with one another. We can now instant message, e-mail, voice mail, fax, phone (landline, satellite, cell, or Internet), walkie-talkie, page, text message, telecommute, or teleconference. Technology is supposed to make life more efficient, productive, and peaceful. Personally, I think the jury's still out on this one.

OK, I admit that if my technology is working right, and if your technology is working right, and if we're each set up with compatible equipment, and if nothing crashes, and if everybody actually knows how to use all this stuff, then yes, in theory, modern communication technology can be enjoyable and productive.

However, let's just suppose (hypothetically, of course) that you take weeks and weeks to get your new office laptop and software coordinated and synchronized with your assistant's PC and software. Your assistant can now sort and prioritize e-mail, categorize and schedule appointments, and handle a lot of your administrative work. Hey! Life is good! The computers are communicating!

Then one day somebody announces cheerfully that new and better options are available. Slicker, more powerful hardware. Superior software. A more user-friendly and efficient interface to boost creativity and effectiveness. Who can argue with progress? Who can resist . . . The Upgrade?

So one morning you arrive at the office and find a sleek new laptop on your desk, featuring new technology, new software, and a whole new calendar and e-mail system. And it certainly does have some great features. There's just one problem. Your computer is no longer on speaking terms with your assistant's computer. These machines can't seem to communicate in the ways that are the most helpful.

What's going on here? Personal computers have been around for quite a while now. If they're continually getting better, why can't they reliably communicate?

It kind of reminds me of marriage. You would think that after years or even decades of being husband and wife, couples might be able to work all the bugs out of the communications process. But it's not that simple. You see, if computers—with chips and buffers and ports and BIOS and files and CPUs and RAM and countless lines of software code and little whirring things and a thousand user options—are complex, then how much more complex are people! And compounding our complexity is the fact that we're sinners. So in every marriage, communication is sure to break down once in a while, sometimes for no obvious reason, and no 24/7 tech rep can help fix it.

In the previous chapter we discussed how relational intimacy is the goal of biblical communication. But how does it all work? What makes for effective biblical communication? How do we get better at it? And why is communication sometimes such a challenge and so confusing?

## Different by Design

Let's start with that last question. Just why *is* communication sometimes such a challenge and so confusing?

Has this ever happened to you? You speak a sentence to your spouse. It's nothing very different, really, from any of the other sentences you speak every day. At the time it seems like your words are clear and familiar, pretty straightforward in their meaning. But then you find out, whether immediately or later, that what your spouse heard bore little resemblance to what you meant.

For example, let's say I call Betsy to tell her I'm packing up to leave the office and will be home shortly. She hears, "You can start putting dinner on the table because packing takes three minutes and the trip home takes seven." Well, at least she used to hear that. But after one cold dinner too many she learned I was really saying, "I have to shut down my computer, clean up all these papers, pack my briefcase, put an envelope in the interoffice mail, and fill the car with gas on the way home, so hold dinner for half an hour." Such miscommunication is surprisingly common, and the results can range from the mildly amusing to the truly problematic. What went wrong?

Well, perhaps nothing actually "went wrong." Perhaps it's just that a very critical component in communication was overlooked: the fact that husband and wife are often quite different from one another. You simply communicate in different ways. These distinctions aren't deficiencies. They are differences, differences designed to fill your relationship with a whole new and expanded way of seeing things. Let's look at three ways such differences can show up.

### *Personal or Impersonal?*

When Betsy and I have couples in our home, the conversation can easily split off in two directions. The women start talking about relationships, children, the home, and things that affect them *personally*. Meanwhile the men might head out to the deck, where they discuss abstract subjects like lawn care, the playoffs, the latest political intrigue, or some new technological toy. The same guys may have hung out on the same deck a dozen times, but they can still talk about the same things. (Guys, maybe you're thinking, *Hey! It's not always the same! The teams change from year to year, and there's always a new gadget.*) Meanwhile, the women are in the living room revisiting essentially the same topics *they* always cover. Oddly enough, we all go away feeling bonded together and relationally enriched.

### *Objective or Subjective?*

A marriage commonly features one spouse (often the husband) who gravitates toward objective facts and observations and one (often the wife) who is most comfortable in the subjective and intuitive. The spouse who loves objectivity will, when communicating, tend to seek data and decisions—"just the facts, ma'am." The one who takes a more intuitive approach may find little satisfaction in facts or opinions that don't convey the emotional or interpersonal heart of a situation.

A husband, for example, may hear about something that has happened and respond briefly with an opinion. He expresses his opinion once, believing once is sufficient. If his wife is the more intuitive spouse, she may not be satisfied knowing his opinion. She wants to know how the news affected him, and she wants *him* to know how the news affected *her*.

When she shares how it affected her, expressing it once may not be enough. Repetition, for her, is a form of emphasis and depth of expression, a kind of emotional identification with what happened that goes beyond a simple matter-of-fact opinion. So, guys, if your wife is repeating something, don't allow yourself to become impatient. With gentleness and genuine interest, find out why it's important to her. You just may find out it should be important to you too.

### *General or Detailed?*

Someone has said that usually men are the headlines while women are the fine print. This is certainly true in our marriage. When I (Gary) hear that someone we know has just had a baby, I ask two questions: "Boy or girl?" and "Is everyone healthy?" That about does it for me. I know if the gift should be pink or blue and how to pray. Is there more?

Apparently a lot more. Because when I mention the birth to Betsy, it invariably triggers a small avalanche of questions.

"What's the baby's name?" (Same as the parents'.)

"Weight and length?" (Small . . . Hey, it's a baby!)

"How long was she in transition?" (Ummm, what's transition again?)

"How long was the labor?" (Just long enough, I guess.)

We've laughed about this fundamental difference between us since we were newlyweds, and this particular illustration is still fresh today.

These categories—personal/impersonal, objective/subjective, and general/detailed—are not exhaustive, and they certainly are not meant to excuse sin, but recognizing them can help us begin to respond to one another with more humility and grace.

At times every husband wishes his wife thought and communicated a little more like he does (and vice versa!). Some husbands even embark on a hopeless, futile quest to remake their wives in their own image. Years ago I heard a man—who obviously had extensive experience in trying to change his wife—share this bit of homespun wisdom: "Not that you'll understand *why* she's thata way, but you can just accept that she *is* thata way. And God *made* her thata way, and you can fast and pray till you don't weigh ten pounds and she'll still *be* thata way." (I'm pretty sure this was the same man I mentioned in Chapter Two who said, "You're gonna want to quit!")

If God has not made men and women to be identical, neither has he made them to be antagonistic. As we mentioned in Chapter Two, he has made them to be complementary: different from each other, but with both being vital. Again, complementary means "that which is required to supply a deficiency," or "the necessary opposite part." Complementary, God-created, man-and-woman relationships appear in their purest form in marriage. From God's perspective, this is "very good."

Within each marriage there is also a second, unique set of factors that don't necessarily arise from the sort of categorical and largely male-female differences described above. These are personal attributes having their source in upbringing, life history, and gifting. They are likewise meant by God to enhance and enrich your life and marriage. In combination, a married couple's complementary and unique differences can produce marked differences in communication style.

Here's the simple truth: Whether due to gender, background, or preferences, our spouse communicates differently than we do. Unless those differences are unbiblical and sinful, we shouldn't try to change that.

When we try, in humility, to address what *sin* has done in our spouse, God approves and extends grace. But when we try to change our spouse into our own image, we stand in opposition to God and miss out on the breadth and depth of fellowship and intimacy that he wants to produce in each marriage.

Every difference in communication style between a husband and wife can be a pitfall or a redemptive platform for change. Whatever your situation, God has handpicked your spouse—with all of his or her unique traits—to complement you in precisely the ways needed to accomplish God's will in your life, in your spouse's life, and in your shared life as a couple. And that includes how the two of you communicate. So if my style includes resisting or refusing my spouse's style, and insisting that my spouse see and say things my way, the result will be poor communication and probably an ever-widening gulf in our marriage. But if I humbly value my spouse as a gift from God, embracing his or her unique perspective and contribution, we will grow both in godliness and oneness.

## VARIETIES OF TALK

Have you ever noticed how many types of conversation occur almost daily in the life of your marriage? A typical conversation on a dinner date can include small talk ("Whoa, I think I'll order what that guy's having"), information exchange ("Did you see that story on the front page of the paper today?"), value sharing ("How should we respond to the Sunday message on evaluating our approach to media and entertainment?"), correction ("Can I offer you a suggestion from our time at your folks' house last week?"), spiritual conversation ("So, what has the Lord been showing you in your devotions lately?"), and self-disclosure ("Can you help me understand why I get so angry with the children?").

A husband and wife who are in tune with each other and are committed to open communication will move naturally together from one type of conversation to another. But as every couple knows, that doesn't always happen. A wife wants to share the burdens of her day, but her husband wants to find out if she paid the credit card bill. A husband wants to get his wife's counsel on a sensitive matter at work; she springs from there to a concern for one of the children. The result is like two people who are in different rooms of the same house, stubbornly intent on staying right where they are, yet trying to have a meaningful conversation by yelling out the windows to each other. It's impersonal, inefficient, and selfish, promotes misunderstanding, and just doesn't make a whole lot of sense. How much better if they humbly agree to join one another in the same conversational place.

Of course, many people simply prefer one type of conversation over others. Some spouses love to talk easily and casually but find it a challenge to express more complex thoughts and feelings. Others have little patience for small talk and find value only in deeper interactions.

The reality is that a marriage needs every type of conversation. For example, effective communication about finances requires small talk ("Did you get the bill payments mailed today?"), information exchange ("Why was the credit card bill so high last month?"), value sharing ("Do you think we have enough life insurance?"), correction ("Can I ask you why you bought that new golf club, given our discussion about the budget last week?"), spiritual conversation ("Do you think the Lord may be calling us to increase our missions giving?"), and self-disclosure ("I'm so tempted to worry about whether we'll be able to pay Junior's college tuition"). To fail to communicate clearly in any one of these ways is to invite miscommunication, misunderstanding, and missed opportunity for genuinely knowing and serving one another.

Ephesians 4:29 is packed with help on the topic of talk: "Let no corrupting talk come out of your mouths, but only such as is good for building up, as fits the occasion, that it may give grace to those who hear." Our words are to be intentional in these three ways: good for building up, befitting the occasion, and giving grace to those who hear. That leaves plenty of room for variety, diversity, and creativity, but it also rules out simply saying whatever I want, whenever I want.

So when I initiate a conversation with Betsy or respond to her desire to talk, I must adopt the mind-set of a servant and be willing to participate (and lead her to participate) in whatever level of fellowship is necessary to understand adequately and to respond appropriately to the topic or issue . . . whether it's mayo or mustard on the sandwich or analyzing a pattern of anger with the children.

## TIME TO TALK

Of course, before you can have biblical communication, you must first begin to communicate. And sin will hinder that too, if you let it. Sin often blocks everyday conversation by showing up in disguise. Let's take a moment to expose a few of the principal ways that can happen, so we can be alert to them, and where necessary repent of them.

### *Laziness Masquerading as Fatigue*

Guys, I don't know about you, but sometimes when Betsy wants to talk, especially at the end of a workday, I can easily find myself saying things like "I can't think of much to say" or "I'm too tired to talk right now" or "I've worked hard all day" (as if she'd spent the day watering the petunias and petting the dog).

The husband is called by God to lead by his example and initiative, and to lead as a servant. Yes, if the husband has had a particularly rough day and the subject matter isn't urgent, maybe the conversation can wait. But that should be the rare exception, not the rule. Remember, husbands, we are to love our wives as Christ loves the Church: humbly and sacrificially. Even when we're tired.

### *Pride Cowering in the Shadows*

I'm a sinner, I admit it . . . in a general sort of way. But what if my spouse wants to talk in detail about raising the kids, or staying within our budget, or why sex hasn't been as good lately, or that checkup I keep putting off, or projects around the house, or unkindness in my speech, or last Sunday's sermon, or reaching out to the neighbors? Well, then I might have to talk about my effectiveness or my failures, and that would lead to talking about my sin in a very specific way! How embarrassing. How much easier it is just to change the subject to something lighter. Or maybe not even talk very much at all.

Are you avoiding conversation because it will expose more of who you really are? That's exactly why you must talk! Never let pride keep you from the relational intimacy and grace that only come through humility.

### *Selfishness Disguised as Inability*

In our counseling experience it's been common for Betsy and me to hear one spouse or the other explain a lack of communication by saying, "That's not my personality," or "Talking isn't one of my strengths," or "That's just the way I naturally am."

Before we cling too tenaciously to the way we "naturally are," let's recall that how we "naturally are" is precisely what sent Jesus to the cross. The Christian life should be a continual process of change and transformation—from what we naturally are to what we are called and empowered to be in Christ—a completely new creation (2 Corinthians 5:17). While making each of us to be unique, God does expect ongoing growth in holiness and godliness. In part, that means serving one another, and in marriage a big part of serving one another involves communication.

## CONTINUING THE CONVERSATION

The ongoing pursuit of fully open and honest biblical communication—humbly spoken and humbly received, through days, weeks, seasons, and years—breathes life, growth, and intimacy into a marriage. God intends for the conversation that began when you two first met to continue with increasing depth and joy, for his glory and your good, until your last word is uttered.

Easier said than done? Absolutely. Even if you and your spouse were not sinners in constant need of God's grace, a thousand mundane daily events would still conspire to disrupt the regular flow of communication between you. Waking up late, unexpected phone calls, some nasty twenty-four-hour virus, the commotion of children, overtime, traffic delays, fatigue, opportunities to serve others—these are just a few of the more common obstacles. How many times have you wanted to throw up your hands and say to your spouse, "E-mail me your calendar, and let's schedule an appointment for next month!"

Yet God's grace is ever-present to help, even when the tide seems to be against us. Here are a few thoughts to help you establish and maintain the flow.

### The Day-to-Day

In what ways do you and your spouse purpose to relate with each other throughout the day? A casual conversation over breakfast, a phone call in the afternoon, a scribbled note on a napkin—these help keep the relationship fresh and growing. It doesn't take three hours of heart-to-heart sharing to let your spouse know, "I'm interested in you. I value your companionship. Among all my relationships, you are God's primary and most precious means of grace to me."

So when your spouse calls you when you are working, view it as an unexpected delight, not an interruption. Nothing on your agenda for that day takes higher priority than communicating with your wife or husband. You don't need to have a lengthy conversation. If you truly can't take much time to talk, it's fine to say so. But never give the signal that this phone call is a bother. And by the way, if your spouse is calling with an urgent need, interrupt what you are doing, and take the time to listen and respond in whatever way is necessary.

Someone has suggested that how you greet each other after having been apart all day can determine the mood in your home for the entire evening. While a cloudy greeting doesn't have to mean a stormy evening, it is true that walking in the door at the end of the day presents a wonderful opportunity.

Here's a tip. While the two of you are apart, anticipate that moment when you're back under the same roof. Imagine the loving embrace, the smile, the kiss, the kind words. Look forward to that moment as a chance to communicate your pleasure at again being together with the one you love. Husbands, if your wife has spent the day caring for young children, she will probably be eager for some adult conversation. Lay down your life, and your newspaper, and lend her your ears. Both of them.

### Busy Seasons

Most marriages pass through one or more seasons (whether days or years in length) when life gets unusually busy. During these times when spontaneous opportunities to communicate become fewer and farther between, planning becomes vitally important. (Here, men, we need to lead and make sure the family calendar is structured around what is primary.) A genuine commitment to communicate will regularly show up on the calendar, written in red. Talk nights, date nights, planning nights, how-about-we-just-lock-the-doors-and-make-love nights . . . they all contribute to that necessary process of ongoing communication.

### *Guard Communication Time Well*

You don't have to do anything exotic or expensive to create communication times. Take a walk. Go for a drive in the country. Share a bag of popcorn or a cup of coffee. You can stay home if you want. The only requirement for effective communication is that your time be uninterrupted: no demands from children, no ringing phones, no bills to pay, no television.

Be especially wary of television, that little square thing (or big rectangular thing) whose seductive glow can suck the life out of a marriage. How much communication time is wasted while we sit glassy-eyed in front of the tube! Folks, if the TV, Internet, or video games are interfering with your communication, do something radical. Consider an entertainment fast for a month for the purpose of developing a new habit of regular conversation and deeper communication.

If the time you've set aside to talk about a particular topic isn't sufficient, schedule another time, or a better time. If your spouse raises an issue you're not prepared to discuss, recommend a specific time when you can return to it in an undistracted way. (Especially in the early years of marriage, it seems that challenging and important subjects often arise late at night, when fatigue compromises our abilities. Ninety minutes past your typical bedtime is usually *not* an ideal opportunity for discussing a delicate or emotion-laden topic.) This will show that you genuinely desire to communicate and aren't just avoiding it. Commit to an alternative time. Just remember: if you put the subject off, you had better not forget to put it back on!

## THE POWER OF ENCOURAGEMENT AND CORRECTION

Scripture directs us to "let no corrupting talk come out of your mouths, but only such as is good for building up, as fits the occasion, that it may give grace to those who hear" (Ephesians 4:29). But how do we match our speech to particular occasions, so that what we say will truly build up our spouse? Thankfully, there are clear biblical guidelines for directing our thoughts and speech. In addition to the practice of spiritual discourse we discussed in Chapter Four, the grace-empowered use of biblical encouragement and correction are practices that belong in every couple's spiritual repertoire.

### *Cultivate the Habit of Biblical Encouragement*

Just as with spiritual discourse, the habit of biblical encouragement doesn't develop spontaneously. In fact, when it comes to encouragement, there's a kind of odd, tragic thing we can do in marriage. When our spouse has a chronic weakness, we can be tempted to withhold encouragement in that area. *I don't want to let my husband think this area is no longer a weakness for him*, a wife might say to herself. *If I encourage him, he might imagine he's arrived and give up trying to change.*

To understand the nature of biblical encouragement, however, is to get beyond this sinful tendency. Biblical encouragement involves actively looking for areas where God is at work in your spouse's life and drawing attention to the grace in operation there. This brings glory to God and hope to both husband and wife. It helps us remember that almost all spiritual change is incremental and that God is always at work to mold us more fully into the image of his Son. The writer of the book of Hebrews considers it so important that he charges us to encourage each other (Hebrews 10:24) and *daily* to exhort one another (Hebrews 3:13).

To encourage someone is to see and rejoice in God's grace being displayed. To withhold encouragement despite progress—even if it's just a glimmer of progress—is to rob God of glory, who is always faithfully at work to conform us to Christ (Titus 2:11-12).

Biblical encouragement recognizes that no true change, however small, can occur apart from the grace of God. There is a real power in being able to see change more from God's perspective and therefore to rejoice at even small improvements.

So look specifically for ways to encourage your spouse, and be gracious and thankful in your receipt of encouragement. You'll be amazed at the way communication thrives in an atmosphere of sincere gratitude and mutual encouragement.

### *Cultivate the Habit of Biblical Correction*

Perhaps you are thinking, *Why this sudden shift from encouragement to correction? Aren't they opposites?*

In a sense, yes, but when you understand the nature of the human heart and God's way of promoting holiness, you see that encouragement and correction are inseparable. None of us ever matures beyond the need for encouragement (because we are still becoming more holy) or correction (because we still sin). Believe me, no matter how much encouragement you may deserve, your spouse will never say, "Congratulations, honey, you've done it. You have attained sinless perfection. There is simply no room left for improvement."

Because spouses should care for and want God's best for each other, grace-filled correction ought to be a desired and active ingredient in every marriage. As the Lord sanctifies us, he calls us to change and bear fruit in areas of attitude, character, and behavior. Often God uses our spouse to spotlight our need for change, and he or she must be willing to serve God's agenda through correction.

Simply stated, in correction your spouse points out either a specific instance of sin or an ongoing pattern of sin in your behavior. The most common sins (in marriage or any other context) involve pride or selfishness in some form.

For most of us, the confrontation that is a necessary component of correction is something we'd rather avoid. It's especially difficult when we suspect our spouse will react defensively or angrily. If your husband or wife often turns hostile or withdraws when you raise a concern, you will be tempted to compromise truth in the interest of maintaining superficial peace. But this is only done at the expense of God's glory and the oneness of marriage. The following counsel from Scripture will help you develop the gentle art of correction in your marriage.

*Learn to humbly seek evaluation, counsel, and correction.* Friends, it is not enough to be willing to be corrected or to wait for correction. Rather, truly fruitful communication only happens when we throw open the doors and say, "Come in—ask anything, look at anything, question anything!" And if no one comes in, we go tell someone what's there. The biblical wisdom made available to us in correction does not appear spontaneously. It does us little good to acknowledge correction grudgingly and half-heartedly or only when it's unavoidable. Rather, we must seek it as treasure.

For example, when I (Betsy) come to Gary because I'm struggling with a burden, concern, or fear, I certainly want him to understand me. But that's just the start. If I'm satisfied with simply expressing how I feel, or even with being better understood, I am not likely to change. I may feel better for a while, but the struggle inevitably returns because the underlying causes remain unchallenged.

It is here that Gary's questions, counsel, care, and correction come into play. As God works through my husband, and as I sincerely desire the treasure of God's wisdom, Gary's words can bring me insight (wisdom for the situation), encouragement (noting where God's grace is at work), correction (helping me see clearly), exhortation (motivating me to a godly response), or even rebuke (a humble, biblical addressing of sin or error).

Do I need understanding from my husband? Yes, but it's God's truth, not Gary's understanding, that ultimately sets me free (John 8:32).

So let your spouse into your life, with no reservations. Open the door wide. It can expose our pride to say to someone who intimately knows our faults and has experienced their effect, "Do you have any questions or concerns about my character, behavior, or thinking that I need to bring to the Lord and others for evaluation?" But it is this very posture that God recognizes as humility. And God's grace flows to the humble (James 4:6; 1 Peter 5:5).

*Make correction part of fellowship, not of conflict.* If your experience of correction has been predominantly negative, please allow this truth to change your thinking. In the Bible, while correction often does bring sin to light, it has its roots in a loving relationship, not in a spirit of judgment, attack, or punishment (Proverbs 27:5-6). The fatherhood of God carries with it the privilege of receiving his correction and discipline as an expression of his love (Hebrews 12:3-11). One characteristic of God's judgment is that he *stops* correcting; instead, he gives people over to their natural inclinations (see Romans 1). Friends, the absence of correction, being left to ourselves, should cause us much alarm and compel us to pursue the evaluation and correction of others.

The willingness to correct biblically is an expression of true love. This makes the relational intimacy of fellowship the ideal context for correction.

*Recognize that correction addresses the chronic problems of human sin and spiritual blindness.* As finite creatures, we are unable to see all we need to. As sinners, we have a selfish disposition to see only what we want to. We are all, to varying degrees, spiritually blind—ignorant of our foolish tendencies and dull to the snares of temptation and idolatry that entangle us. Even as Christians we sometimes "say we have no sin," and thus "we deceive ourselves, and the truth is not in us" (1 John 1:8). Author Paul Tripp has made the sobering observation that the difference between spiritually blind people and physically blind people is that spiritually blind people are typically blind to their blindness![21]

We all have a desperate need for people who can help us see what we can't or won't see on our own. That's the privilege of correction in marriage: we have someone who intimately knows us, helping us to see more clearly in the very areas we most need to see.

*Correct one another out of a desire to serve.* Just as correction ought to be given as part of fellowship, not conflict, it must be performed as an act of servanthood, not judgment. In his Sermon on the Mount, Jesus offers wonderfully clear instruction on how we should, and should not, correct one another.

> *Judge not, that you be not judged. For with the judgment you pronounce you will be judged, and with the measure you use it will be measured to you. Why do you see the speck that is in your brother's eye, but do not notice the log that is in your own eye? Or how can you say to your brother, "Let me take the speck out of your eye," when there is the log in your own eye? You hypocrite, first take the log out of your own eye, and then you will see clearly to take the speck out of your brother's eye.* (Matthew 7:1-5)

Here Jesus warns against judging another's heart, motive, or intentions when we bring correction. Instead, our posture is to be humble and loving, not assuming ill about our spouse. In this way, our spouse benefits from our words, example of humility, and expression of true love.

It pains me (yes, Gary again) to realize how often I can presume to see Betsy's thoughts, motives, and sin clearly when I'm actually looking through the lumberyard of my own arrogance, self-righteousness, and anger. Let's say Betsy didn't make a phone call I asked her to. The same pride that presumes my will should always be done also presumes to know why she didn't make the call. It's only when I've taken a spiritual axe to my own corrupt condition that I can help Betsy with the speck in her eye, if indeed there is one.

## Change Takes Time

As you read this book, we certainly hope you will be motivated to change, and to help your spouse change as well, in a variety of areas. But true character change is hard. In fact, it's impossible without God's grace and a humble heart.

So don't expect change to happen quickly or effortlessly, especially in areas of long-standing difficulty or sin. For most people, the hardest changes involve re-educating one's heart and mind and taming one's tongue. These, of course, are the very areas that cause some of the most persistent and challenging problems in a marriage. Some spouses struggle with deeply entrenched habits of speech like harshness or criticism. For some the sin pattern goes to rage or coarse language. The temptation to insist on obvious, rapid change in areas of greatest weakness (especially in your spouse) can be strong, but don't do it; it's usually foolish and counterproductive. And it's often self-righteous, as if we all don't have besetting sins!

In fact, as you purpose to put into practice what you have learned in this chapter, be sure to begin with yourself. Identify as clearly as you can your own besetting weaknesses and sins. What are your patterns that need God's transforming grace?

I (Betsy) know I have a tendency to finish Gary's sentences for him. Sometimes I interrupt him when he's speaking. He doesn't particularly appreciate such things. Often I jump to conclusions or share how I would have handled a situation differently. None of these things benefits Gary, and I certainly wouldn't want him to communicate the same way with me. So I'm trying to tame my tongue.

Like many husbands, I (Gary) must often resist the urge to provide a quick answer. When Betsy comes to me with a problem, in my pride and arrogance I find it far too easy to say, "Oh, just do this," or "Well, then don't do that." After all, I'm a pastor, and I wrote a book! But what I ought to do at those times is humble myself and *not* do what comes most readily. Instead I must take the time and effort to try to understand Betsy's perspective on what happened. I need to find out not only all the objective details and how she feels, but what she thinks and believes about what happened. We then need to determine if her thoughts are consistent with a biblical perspective of God, his wisdom, and his ways. And guess what—investing a little time to be a patient, loving, and understanding servant with your wife (rather than a proud and self-serving Mr. Fix-it) will prevent hours of conflict.

Well, friends, now which do you think is more complicated—your computer or your spouse? In my pride and arrogance I have repeatedly attempted to "fix" both and found that the bells and whistles of technology pale in comparison to the wondrous intricacies of my wife's heart and soul. And along the way I can still fail to keep a cardinal rule of maintaining or repairing anything: *Read the instructions*. I look at the computer (or camera or cell phone or DVD player). Then I look at the instruction manual, but usually just long enough to decide to wing it. About an hour later, in desperation, I call my oldest son, Garrett, our resident technical problem solver, and in no time the new gadget is operational.

To my regret, I can approach communication with Betsy the same way. I look at our struggling conversation and arrogantly assume, "Nah, I don't need help. I've got this covered." And as you would imagine, about an hour later I humble myself and acknowledge there *is* an instruction manual that will get me to the very root of the problem. It's called the Bible, the Word of God, which perfectly discerns the thoughts and intentions of my heart (Hebrews 4:12). And more often than not, the heart is exactly where the problem lies.

But you don't have to follow my foolishness. By humbly and prayerfully going to Scripture *first*, you can begin to fill your heart and mind with truths that will guide your conversations, guard your speech, and guarantee God's grace for communication—communication that leads to intimacy with one another and conformity to God's Son.

Now . . . that's not so complicated, is it?

*6*

# *The Heart of Conflict*

## RESTORING COMMUNICATION

It was a sad day for Betsy and me when we finally had our 1985 Plymouth station wagon towed to the junkyard. For some time our children had affectionately called it "The Millennium Falcon." If you know the movie *Star Wars* and had seen the car in its old age, you'd understand why. But despite the fact that the hyper-drive was broken (actually, the transmission was shot), we were still sad to lose this old friend, and especially so because of its front bench seat. Remember bench seats? For all those years, Betsy and I had been able to sit close together wherever we went. I'd hold open the driver's door, she would get in, and I'd hop in right after her. Today we have two minivans with bucket seats, and I sure do miss that old car.

But there were times, if we were in the midst of a conflict, that Betsy would get in and slide all the way over to the passenger door. Talk about a picture of how sin separates! I'm sure all married couples can relate. Our physical proximity is often a good gauge of our emotional and relational proximity.

### OUR TRUE PROBLEM

One afternoon, during a counseling session in my office, I couldn't help thinking back to the Plymouth for a moment. The couple sitting across from me looked like they would rather be in separate galaxies, not just separate chairs. Even before a word was uttered, the distance in their body posture clearly indicated an even greater distance in their hearts.

As they began to speak in very controlled and measured words, a familiar story unfolded. She wanted his comfort, affection, and leadership. He wanted her respect, affection, and submission. These are reasonable, godly desires, things the Bible commands husbands and wives to give one another. This couple was accurate in identifying them as legitimate wishes left unfulfilled. In their minds, this was precisely the problem they had come to talk about.

Yet the icy wall between them had not been formed by a failure to fulfill biblical roles. Other problems, ones they could not yet clearly see, had created this separation. In their marriage, as in countless others, the heart of the matter wasn't what each spouse was not getting. The real problem was what they *thought* and *felt* and *believed* about what they were not getting, and how they behaved *as a result* of those thoughts, emotions, and beliefs.

He would come home from work and go right to the computer; she wanted his care and attention. She would often find fault and criticize his decisions; he wanted her enthusiasm and support. They expressed their demands and disappointments with angry and critical words. They had become deeply stuck in a pattern of arrogant anger, harsh language, and selfish withdrawal.

The ultimate reason for their ongoing conflict was not his lack of affection or her lack of submission. Read that again. These certainly were important problems to be addressed, but they did not cause the conflict. So what was the cause? When one spouse was disappointed by the other, the *response* was anger and unkindness rather than love and self-control. And husband and wife each justified his or her sinful response to the other.

You don't have to be married long to be familiar with such conflict. Consider the newlyweds who, while still on their honeymoon, got into such a disagreement that the bride got out of the car . . . while it was moving! The groom had to drive alongside her down the road, pleading with her through the rolled-down window to get back in! Yes, even on a honeymoon! Unbelievable! I won't reveal the names of this couple, but I believe he proposed in a restaurant overlooking Washington, D.C., they would later own a Plymouth station wagon with a bench seat, and I think they even wrote a book on marriage! (Imagine that. There really is grace for growth.)

Newlyweds often panic at their first heated argument. *Nobody told me about this! Did I marry the wrong person? Will this marriage last?* Even seasoned couples can be shaken by an intense dispute. But there's no reason to fear. No matter how long you have been married, disagreement and conflict simply indicate that God is at work, sanctifying and maturing you through the instrument of marriage, making you more like Christ.

## GOD'S SURE SOLUTION

Sin, with all its pride and selfishness, will be with us every day of this life (Jeremiah 17:9; Galatians 5:17; Romans 7:18-19). Certainly, no married couple has ever lived free of conflict. How wonderful, then, that God has given us a clear and certain way of resolving any and all conflicts fully and completely. Husbands and wives can overcome their conflicts through biblical communication, shaped by the power of the gospel.

The gospel reminds us that nothing done *to us*, no matter how wicked, will ever surpass the wickedness done *by us*, to the holy Son of God. While we were still sinners, Christ died for us (Romans 5:8). When the Son suffered on the cross for us, thus resolving the greatest conflict we could ever face—the hatred of a holy God for our sin—he gave us perfect peace with the Father. The perfect resolution of that conflict makes possible the perfect reconciliation of every other conflict, no matter its duration, depth, intensity, or consequences. Our peace with God opens the way to peace in all other relationships.

Resolving conflict is not only possible, it is commanded. "Make every effort to keep the unity of the Spirit through the bond of peace" (Ephesians 4:3, NIV). This chapter is dedicated to the heart and practice of resolving conflict. It is written in the confidence that Jesus the Reconciler will bless and empower our faithfulness as we pursue genuine peace in our marriages. With that firm biblical hope, let's examine what conflict is, what gospel-based resolution is, and how we get from the one to the other.

## CONFLICT'S DEFINITION AND DYNAMICS

Conflict in marriage can take many forms, but the beginning of every conflict is just plain old disagreement. You see something one way, I see it another. Spouses can disagree on almost anything, such as:

- whether to set the thermostat on cool (Gary) or warm (Betsy);
- whether grits are tastier with salt and pepper (Betsy) or sugar (Gary);
- whether to go to the Magic Kingdom (Gary) or World Showcase (Betsy);
- whether to keep stuff (Gary, and all four of our children) or throw stuff away (Betsy);
- whether to watch a dramatic true-to-life movie or escape to a galaxy far, far away (guess!).

Disagreement, debate, and differing desires can enrich marriage by helping us appreciate our spouse's perspective, broadening our view of this great adventure of life together. So why do our disagreements sometimes end in sin and conflict? Let's take a few minutes to find out. A biblical understanding of the dynamics of this process can help us in two ways: we can learn to prevent many conflicts and to repair a relationship damaged by a sinful dispute.

Of course, popular theories about the cause of conflict abound. These include latent psychological urges, mood disorders, negative social conditioning, past emotional trauma, demonic influence, institutionalized injustice, genetic disposition, diet, stress, empty love cups . . . and on and on. Sadly, much of the Christian community has gladly entered into this tempest, becoming engulfed in a swirl of theories that simply can't be reconciled with Scripture. Such theories appeal to our sinful tendency to look somewhere—anywhere—other than our own hearts for the root cause of our sins. So when there's a conflict, we can easily be tempted to see everyone and everything, except ourselves, as blameworthy. Meanwhile, the Scriptures are casually dismissed or conveniently misinterpreted, God's wisdom ignored.

All the while, the Bible makes a bold, clear, and startlingly simple diagnosis of the root cause of conflict. James tackles the subject head-on when he writes:

> *What causes quarrels and what causes fights among you? Is it not this, that* your passions *are at war within you?* You desire *and do not have, so you murder.* You covet *and cannot obtain, so you fight and quarrel. You do not have, because you do not ask. You ask and do not receive, because you ask wrongly, to spend it on* your passions. *(James 4:1-3, emphasis added)*

Here the Bible places the fundamental cause of conflict not in circumstances or misunderstanding or competing ideas, but squarely in the desires, cravings, and passions of *our own hearts*. Disagreements become conflicts because we crave something so much that we will go to war to get it, or will fight to keep someone else from getting what they crave. It is incredibly simple . . . and extremely serious. Here is the general pattern.

### *Desire*

Conflict becomes a possibility when a human heart carries a desire. *I would like him to be more open and take more initiative and leadership in our communication.* Or, *I would like her to understand that sometimes I just don't have a lot to say.*

There is nothing necessarily wrong with either of these desires. So far no sin, no problem.

### *Disagreement/Disappointment*

When our desire meets with disagreement or disappointment, we start to see what sort of hold it has on us. If we say to ourselves, *I can't believe he doesn't want to talk with me right now!* or *Doesn't she realize I'm tired when I come home from work, and just want some time alone!* we have a problem.

Here desire has begun to reveal a craving, lust, or sinful passion. You know the line has been crossed when you are no longer counting your spouse as "more significant than yourselves" (Philippians 2:3).

### *Deserving?*

Our sinful self-orientation begins to look at this unmet desire as something we deserve. *I've been home all day with the children! Don't I deserve his attention and some adult conversation?!* Or, *I've been at work all day solving everyone else's problems! Don't I deserve some peace and quiet?* It's a sure indication we believe our desire is deserved when emotion stirring in our hearts influences the tone or content of our speech.

And so it begins . . .

### *Demanding!*

Once we believe we deserve something, we feel perfectly justified in demanding it. We tack that desire onto our Personal Bill of Rights and get ready to take our case to the highest court in the land. In our defense we might even throw in our own personal interpretation of the Bible. *He's supposed to understand me and meet my need to talk!* Or, *If she was respectfully submissive, she'd give me some space!*

### *Dependence*

Underneath this escalating war, the heart is exposed as depending on the thing desired. It is no longer *I want* or even *I need.* It becomes, *I must have! My peace and joy depend on him talking to me!*—or, *on her leaving me alone!*

### *Deification*

This dependency reveals that we have deified ourselves and our desire. *My kingdom come! My will be done on earth as it is in my imagination!* We elevate ourselves and our cravings to the status of an idol, a false god. We become willing to sacrifice everything—our peace, our obedience, even our spouse—on its altar. We bow to this idol as our source and demand that others bow as well. *Some Christian husband you are! What a hypocrite!* Or, *Some wife! How long since you've read Proverbs 31?*

### *Destruction*

That which our heart deifies eventually destroys our relationships, and us. Of course, the only power a false god has is the power we give it. But when we empower false gods, we turn from the true God and enter into a lie and a destructively foolish way of life. Apart from repentance, idol worship fuels a warfare that becomes a habitual way of living. Like a despot who destroys the nation around him to keep his hold on power, we are willing to lay waste to the very foundation of our marriage in order to satisfy our deified cravings.

The picture isn't pretty. But, with perhaps a few minor variations, it precisely explains from a biblical perspective not only the epidemic abomination of divorce among confessing Christians, but the less violent tragedy of bankrupt marriages all around us.

Sometimes the pattern of escalation I've described takes place gradually over months or years. Some couples have trod such a well-worn path that they move from Desire to Destruction almost instantly, over virtually any disagreement, with nearly every conversation becoming a conflict. Perhaps your marital disputes haven't quite taken you to the edge of that abyss. But you must take seriously the escalating power of this pattern. And you must ask God to help you identify the sin that takes control in your heart whenever you can't keep emotion from entering the disagreement.

## Conflict's Degrees and Disguises

Discovering the biblical roots of conflict requires that we recognize the many forms of conflict—some subtle, and some obvious. We all have met couples who say, "We never argue." Scratch below that statement, however, and you're likely to find a fairly narrow definition of conflict.

Perhaps in some cases you don't argue, you just withdraw (a refusal to deal with a sinful attitude). If you and your spouse have "healthy debates" (lasting for days), you would do well to observe the "bite and devour" warning in Galatians 5:15. Consider also the term "strife" in 1 Corinthians 3:3 (a chronic undercurrent of contention) and "discord" in Galatians 5:20 (an inability to find harmony on a certain point). A lack of volume in my speech or anger on my face doesn't necessarily mean the absence of sin and conflict in my heart.

One good way to identify conflict is to see it not so much in the presence of something, but in the absence. If the biblical goals of marriage are increasing oneness and holiness for the glory of God, then a lack of growth in these areas almost certainly indicates some underlying conflict. So if, for example, a husband and wife are unable to have biblical fellowship, or if they will not pursue intimacy, a conflict is clearly involved, no matter what has been said or not said.

## Conflict's Point and Purpose

Because God is sovereign and ever at work for our good and our growth in godliness, conflict can always be redemptive. The storms of conflict actually test how we're building our marriages. You can think of conflicts as spiritual pop quizzes from God.

It seems God often lets me (Gary) be caught off guard. I can't count the number of times that just when I think I might have this husband thing figured out, it happens: "Okay, Mr. Maturity, Mr. Understanding, Mr. Love That Lasts—it's quiz time!" And soon, a few minutes into another unexpected conflict, I realize I'm either blaming Betsy for it or am trying to excuse, justify, or explain away my own sin.

Who enjoys tests? But they are indispensable to our sanctification and the display of God's glory through our lives. First of all, they are essential in providing a realistic assessment of the condition of our marriage. Conflict, especially the unexpected kind, helps reveal the weaknesses in our marriage and the temptations in our hearts. The better we know these weaknesses, the more we will be able to apply the grace of God toward the overcoming of sin.

Second, every disagreement is an opportunity for husbands to demonstrate servant leadership—to take initiative, exercise self-control, practice listening, and discern the best course of action. Meanwhile, the wife can develop her ability to respond with trust, respect, and self-control.

Third, conflict exposes our pride and the power of our sin, reminding us of our desperate need for the grace, mercy, and wisdom of God. Conflict sends the humble Christian to prayer and enrolls the proud Christian in the school of humility. Humility, in turn, positions us to receive God's grace (James 4:6; 1 Peter 5:5) to improve our marriage at its points of weakness.

All conflicts in a marriage can be resolved. *Yes, all.* Our God is able to resolve them. Therefore, any resignation, despair, or hopelessness you may feel regarding your marriage stems far more from an inadequate view of God than it does from any view, accurate or inaccurate, of your spouse or yourself.

Because of God's particular love for us, conflict resolution is not just a means to a narrow, particular end. It is an opportunity to grow in sanctification, to glorify God more completely, and to build trust and deepen love at the heart of the marriage. But where do we begin?

## THE PATH TO PEACE

Having given attention to what makes up conflict, let's turn to what makes up conflict *resolution*. How do we get from fighting and quarreling to a true, godly peace? Well, what started the war? (Hint: refer back to James 4.) Right!—my passions, lusts, desires, and cravings, and how I responded when they were not satisfied. Resolving conflict begins with seeing the reality of sin in my heart, the sin that so often turns disagreement into conflict.

Often when we are in the midst of conflict, our sinful desires point us toward one overriding goal: *victory for me, and unconditional surrender for you!* Have you ever reflected on a recent conflict and realized you had expended great energy and effort trying to prove some ultimately insignificant point? Or that you had argued passionately for a firm position on a secondary matter when a little compromise would have settled everything just fine? Why do we do that? Simple: we want to *win*. To be proven right, vindicated, our moral or intellectual superiority plainly established—at the other person's expense. So winning (not serving, honoring, or pleasing God) is often my chief goal in a conflict. I want to be God!

Let's go for another ride in the car with Gary and Betsy. This happened several years ago at a busy intersection. Because we drove on this street frequently, we knew the intersection had a "No Turn on Red" sign. But on this particular day I (Gary) noticed that the sign had been removed. So I stopped for the red light, looked for oncoming traffic, and made the turn.

Betsy panicked. "Dear," she said, "you can't turn on red here!"

Instead of explaining or saying something kind and reassuring, I let pride well up in my heart, producing a quiet, determined, sinful anger. To think she would accuse me, with my impeccable driving record and skill, of doing something as stupid as running a red light! So in arrogant, vengeful silence, I drove all the way around the block and came back to the light.

"Look," I declared in triumph, "no sign!"

There. I had established my superiority in the face of this baseless claim. My pride was raging, and I felt really good—for about ten seconds.

Then a wave of convicting guilt washed over me.

I had tried to shame my own wife. I had humiliated her, and in a wicked way I had enjoyed it! I wasn't really trying to resolve anything when I went around the block. I was just trying to win. I was proud. Had I been humble, I would have taken the time to explain my actions and allay her fears. To reassure her, I might even have shown her—with a humble heart instead of a haughty one—that the sign really was gone. But I just wanted to defend myself, to prove I was right. I wanted her to decrease so I could increase. I wanted her to worship me—my driving ability and my acute powers of observation. But all I had done was put on display my selfish, foolish, self-righteous arrogance.

Thankfully, the Bible offers a conclusion to conflict, one infinitely more satisfying than self-exaltation. It offers the way to peace—genuine, godly, harmonious peace. The peace God has granted to us—peace with himself through the reconciling work of Jesus on the cross—is meant to be actively in play as we resolve conflicts with one another. As Paul writes to the church in Corinth, "Finally, brothers, rejoice. Aim for restoration, comfort one another, agree with one another, live in peace; and the God of love and peace will be with you" (2 Corinthians 13:11).

### *What Peace Is Not*

So what is this biblical peace that Paul refers to? North Korea and South Korea can be said to be "at peace," but it takes barbed wire, land mines, and vigilant troops to maintain it. Whenever two boxers retire to their respective corners of the ring between rounds, there is an interlude of something resembling peace. But clearly, true peace is far more than the absence of active conflict.

At the same time, peace is not permanent, unbroken relational serenity. It is not a destination at which we can arrive. The Bible never suggests that conflict will be utterly banished from any aspect of this life. In fact, the Bible assumes the ongoing need for peace*making* because we will all sin until we die.

### *What Peace Is*

Biblical peace is therefore a lifelong focus, a process, a journey, a heart attitude, a matter of regular and careful attention. In its progressive, ongoing nature, peace is a lot like sanctification, to which it is inextricably bound.

So in marriage, genuine peace does not mean the absence of all conflict. It means that when conflicts arise, they are handled and resolved biblically because loving, pleasing, and honoring God is reestablished as our greatest desire and pursuit. Biblical communication is resumed and relational intimacy restored. If all offenses are resolved after a conflict, then peace is maintained, even if a legitimate disagreement or difference of opinion remains.

Peacemaking is intended to be a two-way street, requiring the commitment of both spouses. Now, if I refuse to make peace with Betsy after a conflict, she can still fully please God by interacting with me—despite my arrogant posturing—in humility and love (and obviously this also applies if the roles are reversed). But to consistently resolve conflict in marriage, both husband and wife must be committed to peacemaking.

### *Humble Recognition of Sin*

Peacemaking begins with me being able to recognize and acknowledge my own sin, and that takes humility. Humility makes me more focused on *my* sin than on my spouse's (see Matthew 7:1-5). If I'm being humble, I won't assume or judge or blame-shift or require my spouse to acknowledge his or her sin before I acknowledge my own. I'll resist the urge to blame my spouse for my sinful reactions. (He or she may *tempt* me to a sinful response, but God holds me accountable for the response itself.) I'll admit that perhaps I don't see things as clearly as I should. And I'll be open to the idea that maybe, just maybe, my spouse is right!

When I see my own sin and sinfulness in light of God's mercy to me, I can gently and patiently press a peacemaking conversation to resolution. I can search my *own* heart, letting God search my spouse's. I won't manipulate with anger or silence, and if my spouse attempts to do so, rather than giving up or giving in to judgmental bitterness, I can forbear (Ephesians 4:31-32).

Forbearance is not just tolerance. It is a commitment, grounded in faith, to love a fellow sinner in full acknowledgment of his or her unconfessed sin. It is an active and sometimes difficult decision to respond to sin with mercy, in the confidence that God is always at work in the heart of your spouse. Committing yourself to serve in the sanctification process over time is not to ignore or excuse your spouse's sin. It is to recognize that the Spirit of God generally brings illumination, understanding, and conviction *gradually*. Humble patience in a conflict echoes the long-suffering nature of God's love for us.

### *Biblical Confession of Sin*

It is not enough for me just to *see* my sin. I must also *confess* it. Regardless of what's going on between me and my spouse, sin is first of all against God (Psalm 51:3-4). When I'm in a conflict, I desperately need God's help, but my sin offends him. If I'm unwilling to confess my sin (regardless of the seriousness of my spouse's offense), God will oppose me in my pride. God is far more concerned about whether I am humble than whether I am right.

We don't need to *feel* like we have sinned to *know* we have sinned. God's Word evaluates our actions and motives for us (Hebrews 4:12). And we don't need to be experiencing guilt to make our confession valid. Yes, an appropriate emotional sensitivity to one's sin is a good thing, for godly sorrow leads to repentance (2 Corinthians 7:10). However, while we never want to be casual about sin, effective confession and genuine forgiveness do not require deep emotion.

If we are thinking, doing, or feeling anything contrary to what God has revealed for us in his Word, we have something to confess. And because every conflict involves two sinners, no conflict should end without each person asking God to reveal his or her own specific sin that needs to be confessed, to God and to each other.

Biblical confession cuts to the core of the matter. It agrees with God and his Word about my sin. It puts God's reality on the table for all to see. But biblical confession must take a biblical form.

*Biblical confession is specific.* "I'm sorry I hurt you" is neither specific nor a confession. "Would you please forgive me for my unkind speech that revealed sins of anger, selfishness, and pride" may sound awkward at first, but language like this, honestly and humbly spoken, is vital to true biblical confession.

To own the full weight of your sin, use biblical words and categories and terms that really speak to what is going on in the heart. Don't confess to being "frustrated" or "preoccupied." Call sin what it is. Frustration is a form of anger (from not getting your way—see James 4:1-4), and preoccupation is a symptom of an underlying selfishness that fails to look out adequately for the interests of others (Philippians 2:3-4). Charles Spurgeon writes, "Do not give fair names to foul sins; call them what you will, they will smell no sweeter. What God sees them to be, that do you labour to feel them to be; and with all openness of heart acknowledge their real character."[22]

*Biblical confession is unqualified.* Confession is not an opportunity to present a "balanced" analysis of the conflict. Confession is about *your* sin, period. Don't use your confession to list your partner's faults: "I was wrong, but . . ." That three-letter word negates the impact of anything else you might say.

*Biblical confession is sincere.* Even if we have to preface our confession with something like "I really don't think I see all of my sin yet in this area," or "I don't feel what I should be feeling about my sin at the moment," we can still confess sin clearly and sincerely, trusting God to reveal more later. Often conviction and sorrow come on the heels of humble confession. Puritan pastor Thomas Watson wrote:

> Our hearts must go along with our confessions. The hypocrite confesses sin but loves it, like a thief who confesses to stolen goods, yet loves stealing. How many confess pride and covetousness with their lips but roll them as honey under their tongue. Augustine said that before his conversion he confessed sin and begged power against it, but his heart whispered within him, "not yet, Lord."[23]

Once we grasp the biblical truth that "God opposes the proud, but gives grace to the humble" (James 4:6), then whenever we become aware that our sin has contributed to a conflict in any way, biblical confession is the only appropriate response. A biblically informed confession of sin prepares the way for forgiveness and fellowship—a far better place than a cold night in separate rooms!

### *Complete Forgiveness of Sin*

If I have just confessed my sins, my next step is to request forgiveness. This is no small thing. It isn't like two preschoolers who've just gotten into a tussle scuffing their feet and looking at the floor as Mom says, "Johnny, tell Mikey you're sorry for taking the last cupcake. Mikey, tell Johnny you forgive him. Now hug and go outside."

Scenes not too different from that one are acted out by adults every day in the name of conflict resolution. But forgiveness is not just an exchange of stock phrases so we can go back to playing together nicely. Forgiveness is one of the richest concepts in the Bible. To know Christ is to be forgiven. The cross is the cost of our forgiveness. It is clearly important to our forgiving God that his children likewise treat forgiveness as a serious matter.

Author Ken Sande, in his most helpful book *The Peacemaker*, writes:

> To forgive someone means to release from liability to suffer punishment or penalty . . . forgiveness is undeserved and cannot be earned . . . forgiveness requires that you absorb certain effects of another person's sins and release the person from liability to punishment. This is precisely what Jesus accomplished at Calvary. He secured our forgiveness by taking on himself the full penalty of our sins (Isa 53:4-6; 1 Peter 2:24-25). Remembering what he did to purchase our forgiveness should be our greatest incentive to release others from the penalties they deserve.[24]

Jesus taught that a willingness to extend forgiveness is a mark of a true disciple. Forgiveness is a necessary element of biblical conflict resolution. Here are some things to remember when it is time to seek or grant forgiveness.

*Seeking forgiveness.* We must *ask* for forgiveness—plainly, clearly, and without qualification. Do not assume it just happens. And seek it as a needy one coming with a request, not as a deserving one bringing a demand. To ask for forgiveness half-heartedly is to invite bitterness and mistrust into the relationship.

If your request for forgiveness is not honored quickly and eagerly, recognize that your sin may have made it more difficult to extend genuine forgiveness. (Recognize also that a response of impatience or anger on your part reveals a lack of humble sincerity in your request.) Far better to be forgiven truly rather than instantly but incompletely.

*Granting forgiveness.* When your spouse seeks your forgiveness, be committed to granting it. Jesus doesn't give us the option not to.

To extend forgiveness is a precious thing. The one who forgives expresses a willingness to cancel debts, and even to absorb some of the bad fruit of the other person's sin against him or her. To forgive means to commit myself to not bring up that person's forgiven sin in my thoughts, words, or actions toward him or her at any point in the future for the purpose of accusation. As with a half-hearted request for forgiveness, the half-hearted granting of it likewise reveals bitterness and mistrust.

The granting and extension of forgiveness creates a lasting reconciliation and converts a destructive event into a redemptive one. This process echoes the gospel and is only possible because of the gospel. "Conflict always provides an opportunity to glorify God, that is, to show him honor and bring him praise. In particular, conflict gives you a chance to show God that you love, respect, and trust him. At the same time, it allows you to show others that God is loving, wise, powerful, and faithful."[25]

*Follow-up.* At some point after every conflict there should be a humble, peaceful discussion about what happened. The goal is to identify necessary areas of ongoing repentance, the turning from old ways to pursue a new course of action and thinking.

Sometimes this can take place immediately after the conflict, but often it's best to wait a bit. Betsy and I have built a habit of reviewing our conflicts within a day or two of resolving them. For us, by this time there is generally a clearer understanding of our sin and its effects.

Far from contradicting the principle of leaving forgiven sin in the past, the follow-up process enables us to further humble ourselves, understand each other, and if necessary resolve the issues more completely. It also solidifies our intent to be more understanding and less selfish in the future. If we approach conflict resolution not just as the welcome end to a problem or unpleasant experience but as an opportunity to grow—which is God's intention—we will plan steps of repentance and change.

When we truly and accurately recognize our sin, confess it, and seek forgiveness for it in the light of the gospel, we will be making "every effort" to resolve whatever separates us (Romans 12:18, NIV). When we refuse to settle for less than complete reconciliation and commit to taking whatever time or help is needed to get there, we will be indeed living by Paul's injunction to the Ephesians:

> *I therefore, a prisoner for the Lord, urge you to walk in a manner worthy of the calling to which you have been called, with all humility and gentleness, with patience, bearing with one another in love, eager to maintain the unity of the Spirit in the bond of peace. (Ephesians 4:1-3)*

## The Role of the Church

What if we just keep going around in circles, arguing over the same things in the same way? What if my particular sin pattern is so deep, I don't respond to resolution or reconciliation? What if we reach an impasse in our efforts to resolve a conflict, with neither person willing to budge or admit fault?

Yes, sometimes a couple can just get stuck in sin, ignorance, and pride. And this is one of the many reasons God has given Christians the gift of one another—in the form of the local church. Active, meaningful involvement in the fellowship of a local church under godly, mature pastoral care offers us the loving, biblical wisdom we need to help us extract ourselves from ruts of conflict and get on the path of reconciliation.

As I (Betsy) stated in Chapter Three, I so admire how Gary has made himself accountable in this way. He has made it clear that if I ever feel he's not responding to a conflict, or if it's lasting too long, I have complete liberty to ask appropriate church leadership to get involved. And he has assured me he won't see this as betrayal or as resisting or usurping his authority. This is one way I can be a helper to his leadership, and it shows me that Gary really cares about our marriage, really loves me, and is humble enough to know he's far from infallible. He is willing to open our conflicts up to others, if necessary, to prevent the damage that can be caused by stubborn pride or prolonged disobedience.

I (Gary) want to add that I'd be a fool to live any other way. I know because I've done so. The Bible is too clear, and my sin is too real, to make myself the final judge of how my marriage is doing. So let me urge you to make sure your wife has the same understanding Betsy does. And then go the next step. Make a commitment that if any aspect of your marriage needs attention, you will be the first to seek help from your church.

Humbling yourself before others takes real faith and positions you to receive life-transforming grace. God has established his church knowing that for us to become like him, we need each other. Every couple should prayerfully seek and get actively involved in a local church where the pastors demonstrate and uphold the joy and sanctity of covenant love in marriage. And every couple should have another couple with whom they can share anything and everything. Please don't neglect this. This is certainly another application of the biblical principle that "two are better than one" (Ecclesiastes 4:9).

## GETTING BETTER EVERY YEAR

Here again is the overarching perspective to keep in mind before, during, and after conflict: it is meant for our good.

When we successfully resolve a disagreement, we're doing far more than avoiding a storm. By the Spirit, we're putting sin to death. We're growing closer to one another and becoming more like Christ. As God uses conflict and communication to change us, we won't have to face some of the same old sin issues year after year.

Conflict resolution also draws us closer to each other, resulting in deeper levels of understanding, humility, and intimacy. Each conflict biblically, thoroughly, and happily concluded deepens our marriage union.

So many couples spend their lives avoiding conflict. They choose a superficial "peace at any price"—a price much higher than they realize.

Acknowledging sin, confessing sin, asking forgiveness, and repenting of the sin that leads to conflict is humbling, challenging, and can be painful. But in the end it brings the grace of God and the restoration of harmony and relational intimacy.

Betsy and I have had the privilege of serving so many couples who through grace, faith, and obedience have turned from strife and misery to harmony and intimacy. God is faithful, and there is no situation beyond his ability to restore when both partners want to do God's will. Let that stir great hope and anticipation in your own hearts.

As we close this chapter, I'd love to say I just went out and bought some classic car with a bench seat. (I once had a 1967 Plymouth Belvedere II that would be perfect . . .) But sadly, no. The family still has two minivans with bucket seats, and that makes sitting close to Betsy, at least physically, simply out of the question.

But you know, bucket seats or not, we've never been closer or more intimate in our hearts. God has mercifully shown us that because of the gospel of grace, we can more clearly see our sin, confess our sin, and forgive and be forgiven of our sin. So our testimony today, like that of so many other couples, is that we are closer, reconciliation is quicker, restoration sweeter, and the grace of God more real than ever.

# 7

# It Never Has to Get Old

## THE SOUL OF ROMANCE

Ah, romance! Prior to marriage we dream about it, think about it, and fantasize that it will characterize our every waking moment as a married couple. Then one day we meet that special someone and pursue courtship. Our feelings are all so alive and new! We propose marriage, and she says yes, and our emotions soar! We talk for hours on the phone and can't wait to see one another again! The wedding day finally arrives, followed by a honeymoon of wondrous bliss—certainly a foretaste of a glorious "happily ever after!"

Then we return home, and slowly but relentlessly the constant and inescapable heat of daily life gradually evaporates the refreshing dew of romance. Complacency slowly smothers consistency. Excitement is eroded by "expected." And "I can't wait to . . ." gets squeezed into "I have to . . ." or "I don't have time to . . ."

What happened? Was the hope of lifelong, increasingly passionate romance in marriage just an illusion? Is it really possible to love one another more deeply with each passing year? Does God actually concern himself with committed, romantic love?

For answers to these questions we need look no further than the Bible, the Word of God.

## GOD OF LOVE, GOD OF ROMANCE

Our God, you see, isn't just interested in love. He *is* love (1 John 4:16). He defines love, and he gives love as a gift to his creation, including romantic love between a husband and wife.

### *Romance Is Biblical*

Although the word *romance* does not appear in the Bible, Scripture offers several powerfully inspiring examples of passionate love between a man and a woman. The Old Testament speaks of the poignant, redemptive love of Boaz for Ruth (Ruth 2:8-16; 3:8-13) and of Jacob's passion for Rachel (Genesis 29:20). The entire book of the Song of Solomon is devoted to the magnificent and wondrous love relationship between a man and a woman. And the New Testament warns husbands and wives against physical separation, except briefly for spiritual reasons (1 Corinthians 7:5) and speaks of husbands "nourishing" and "cherishing" their wives (Ephesians 5:29). Appropriate romantic affections and actions are found throughout God's Word; so we can confidently cultivate them in our marriages.

### *Romance Enhances Intimacy*

There is a mysterious experience of becoming one that is unique to biblical marriage. A husband and wife who stand before God in the covenant of marriage as sinners saved by grace possess the potential for a depth of intimacy that no other relationship can touch. It is an intimacy that clearly involves the physical, but much more as well—an intimacy of heart and mind, of spirit and vision, of faith and hope. No marriage in this fallen world is all it could be. Yet all Christian marriages have this extraordinary potential, with romance as a crucial catalyst.

### *Romance Is Exclusive*

"Therefore a man shall leave his father and mother and hold fast to his wife, and the two shall become one flesh" (Ephesians 5:31). There is no place for feelings of romance outside of your marriage.

### *Romance Is an Art*

There is no such thing as a romance expert or passion professional. Romance must be continually practiced, like an art. The basic tools that you as a budding artist must bring to your craft include a heart of humility, a spirit of servanthood, a biblical understanding of marriage, and a fervent desire to know and love your spouse as consistently and creatively as possible. As you put those tools to good use, you will marvel at the new experiences and expressions of romance you can enjoy together. We will spend the rest of this chapter finding out how to make that happen, by God's grace.

## Pursue Romance with Passion

In this section we'll draw some lessons from the Song of Songs (also known as the Song of Solomon). If you've never read this book of the Bible, please make it a priority soon. But be warned, it is not like any other book. It is a God-inspired book of covenant commitment and sensual passion in the context of betrothal and marriage. So we don't suggest, for example, reading it to one another while driving in the car or for family devotions. It's far better to read it in one sitting with your spouse close by. What an opportunity to be not merely hearers of God's Word but doers (James 1:22).

(At this point I, Gary, must recommend a great companion volume by my dear friend C.J. Mahaney. It's called *Sex, Romance, and the Glory of God: What Every Christian Husband Needs to Know*. On the glorious topic of romance in marriage, the book is as clear, concise, and creative as you could ask for. And, guys, the subtitle is not hype. We *need* to know this stuff. In fact, reading and applying that book is one of the best gifts you could give your wife.)

Betsy and I have studied the Song of Songs together. And one of the many things that makes the Song so wonderfully accessible and inviting, as we read the book, is that it is the story of an ordinary couple, like you, like us, who experience the joy and triumph of romance in the midst of everyday circumstances and challenges.

What follows is not a theological exposition. We're just trying to draw out a few instructive and inspiring points for application. As you read this chapter, we invite you to open your Bible to the Song, review the passages we refer to, and as you see how deeply this couple loves one another ask God's Spirit for creative ideas for application in your own marriage.

### *Complete Commitment and Unwavering Allegiance*

This is not a couple in love with love. Instead, they cherish being specifically and uniquely joined to one another. "My beloved is mine, and I am his," she proclaims (2:16).

The goal in marriage is to train your attractions, affections, and desires to fit only one person. It is imperative that your spouse know that no other person or image enters your mind when romantic feelings flood your heart. Romance calls for passionate loyalty—a marriage union defended at all costs. When asked, "What is your beloved more than another . . .?" this woman launches into a detailed description and defense of him (5:9-16). May we be as zealous in our loyalty and commitment.

### *Eager Anticipation and Thrilling Thoughts of Affection*

Passion has a delightfully distracting quality to it. It makes the mind drift, even tumble, into thoughts about our beloved. Listen to the longing of the country maid for her beloved: "Let him kiss me with the kisses of his mouth! For your love is better than wine" (1:2).

When passion is rightly focused, the *only* thoughts that stir passion are thoughts of our spouse. "I will seek him whom my soul loves" (3:2). Such thoughts of one another feed a strong, healthy, God-glorifying passion. A warm glow of fondness when apart is then easily fanned into flaming desire when together. And fostering our thoughts and affections for one another protects us from allowing our thoughts to drift elsewhere. "If you find my beloved . . . tell him I am sick with love" (5:8). Do your hearts yearn for one another? They can. Read on.

### *Communicating with Carefully Crafted Words*

In a marriage rich with romance, love compels us to communicate through words, whether verbally or in writing. There should be something marvelously unique about the way you communicate with your spouse through words, words you don't say or write to anyone else. We must verbally express our love in personal ways, in private and in public. This involves studying our spouse and extolling what we see, stretching our vocabulary to its limits. "Behold, you are beautiful, my love, behold, you are beautiful! Your eyes are doves behind your veil" (4:1). "My beloved is radiant" (5:10). We don't need to be poets, but let's learn how to speak words of romance that will be meaningful to our beloved.

Note here what C.J. Mahaney says about the poetic compliments found in the Song:

> When the man says, "All beautiful you are, my darling; there is no flaw in you" (4:7, NIV), and when he calls her, "my perfect one" (6:9), what's going on is very clear. He is lavishing high praises upon his beloved in an effort to communicate her effect on him. These are expressions of his heartfelt evaluation of her. They are not based on cultural criteria. Others may not share his assessment of her beauty, but he doesn't care. This is how he sees her, and together they rejoice in that assessment.[26]

### *Affection, Touching, and Being Close*

Touch is a language in itself, from a reassuring "I enjoy loving you" to an unmistakable "I love enjoying you." The couple in the Song of Songs loved to be close. Their affection could be passionate and aggressive: "When I found him whom my soul loves . . . I held him, and would not let him go" (3:4) And it could be tender and gentle: "Who is that coming up from the wilderness, leaning on her beloved?" (8:5). So hold hands; greet with a hug and a kiss—and kiss anytime! Our children (now older) still feign embarrassment when Betsy and I are affectionate. "Uh . . . you don't want to go in the kitchen. They're having a romantic moment in there."

A word of warning: Touching can too easily be selfishly motivated. (Are you listening, guys?) Don't use touching as merely a way to get your spouse to the bedroom. That's not affection—it's manipulation. Let's seek to make touching part of our lifestyle as couples, not just an occasional means to an end.

## Protect Romance as Treasure

In the Song of Songs the maiden makes a request of her beloved: "Catch the foxes for us, the little foxes that spoil the vineyards, for our vineyards are in blossom" (2:15). Her concern is that these "little foxes" will raid the vineyards just when the vines are most beautiful. Figuratively speaking, she is concerned that the intimacies of marriage will be spoiled if not protected. What are some of the "little foxes" we need to watch out for in order to protect the tender vine of romance in marriage?

### *Ignorance*

No bride or groom leaves the wedding or honeymoon an expert in romance. As sinners, we all come to marriage with mixed motives, uncertain expectations, and usually novice-like techniques. Men are taught by the secular culture to equate romance with lust, and women are taught to equate romance with feelings. Both approaches sell a lot of movies and novels, but neither helps romance blossom. We must each bring to marriage the heart of a humble, eager, and determined learner.

So talk to trusted and mature friends. Seek their counsel and their recommendations on helpful materials. Most importantly, ask your spouse how he or she defines romance. What touches the soul? What stirs the affections and passions? What's simply enjoyable? Here is the not-so-secret key to ending your ignorance: ask!

### *Selfishness*

Very often the enemy attacking the vine of romance is simple, sinful selfishness. And it often hides behind excuses like forgetfulness or fatigue. Selfishness uses romance to manipulate a spouse—for example, to get sex or attract attention—in loving pursuit of *me*. Selfishness neglects romance if it seems inconvenient or unfulfilling. Selfishness is still passionate, but for the wrong things.

### *Busyness*

This is one of the slyest foxes in any garden. Busyness that regularly crowds out romance is a type of selfishness, a failure of priority. Busyness is loving something more than God or my spouse.

You might protest, *Wait a minute! Do you think I love the overtime that wears me out or the laundry that has to get done!*

The issue is one of priorities and choices. What do you see as essential—really, truly essential? In the final analysis we always do what we do because of a desire . . . either a desire to get something or to avoid something. In either case, what we do reveals what we most want.

Do your calendar, budget, and conversation demonstrate that romance is a priority for you? We all know that romance can tend to fall by the wayside and ultimately get run over by other things. Although romance includes very deep and desirable emotions, it does not just happen automatically and effortlessly. When it comes to the things truly important to us there is no, "We'll get around to it when we can." If romance is a priority, we will make time for it. If it isn't, we won't. That's how you tell if something is truly a priority. What we deeply value, we will make happen.

Men, we can help our wives deal with their busyness. Recognize that other than God the most permanent person in your wife's life is you. Especially if she is a mother and homemaker, her world is constantly in transition. The clothes get washed and then soiled again. The dishes get clean, then dirty. The children in whom she invests so much will one day be gone. Change may be her only constant—besides God and you. Purpose to be, in her life, a constant source of loving leadership, romance, and support.

As a full-time mother of four, I (Betsy) often drift toward putting the needs of the kids ahead of Gary's. Why? Because I'm with them *all the time!* And now that they're older, in some ways the demands become even greater. Yet it's vital that I understand the limits on my relationship with them. They will always be my children, but my role is to raise them so they will go out and fulfill God's purpose for their lives. Gary, on the other hand, intends to stay. My relationship with him should continue to grow for as long as we both shall live. The most important thing a mother can do for her children is to love their father.

My brother demonstrated this spouse-first principle years ago, and it continues to have an impact on us. A friend was noting how delightful C.J.'s daughter was, suggesting to C.J. that surely she must be the apple of his eye. Without a moment's hesitation C.J. pointed to his wife, Carolyn, and said, "No, I love my daughter, but *she* is the apple of my eye." May each of us treasure our spouse like that.

### *Bitterness*

A subtle but deadly attack on romance sometimes comes from bitterness. Bitterness is that deep root that has allowed disappointment, unmet expectations, offense, or unforgiveness to deceive us into believing we didn't get what we deserved, or got what we didn't deserve. Bitterness passes judgment on others, including God, because of their failure to satisfy some desire we have deified in our hearts. Bitterness is so wicked because of the self-righteous judgment that sees the faults and failures of others as exceeding our own. And it results in a failure to forgive others as we have been forgiven.

Friends, the cross of Jesus Christ reminds us that none of us should *want* what we actually deserve (the wrath of God), and the gospel reminds us that mercifully, if we are Christians, we won't ever *get* it.

When affected by bitterness, we withdraw, neglect and avoid our spouse, caress and compliment less, and criticize more. If this is you, you must go to the cross and consider God's mercy and grace toward you, a sinner who needs the Savior every bit as much as anyone else. Confess your bitterness as self-righteous sin against God. Then pursue humble, open, and redemptive conversation with your spouse. Let God rekindle your care and affection for one another.

### *Pride*

Another predator in our garden of marriage is sinful pride that can take two different forms. The first asks no questions because it sees no needs. It may be mixed with ignorance, but in the final analysis it is highly self-confident and self-reliant. This is the guy who says, "I'm all over this romance thing. My wife is one lucky lady." At the other extreme is a pride that sees the need for help, but so craves the reputation of really knowing about romance, it is too fearful—too proud—to ask.

Both enemies are willing to sacrifice romance on the altar of self-importance. For a husband, this little fox is often quickly driven off simply by inviting your wife to evaluate your pursuit of romance and asking for her help to cultivate romance. How many gardens would be spared by this simple step of humility!

Little foxes thrive where our hearts and attention are divided. Why not take a walk together around the garden of your marriage and see if there might be some predators that need to be run off? Go through the list provided here and then ask yourselves: what is getting the attention and affection that should be going to our romance?

## Practice Romance as an Art

As an art major in college, I (Gary) had to take a ceramics class. I remember approaching a potter's wheel for the first time, expecting to sit down and turn out a beautiful piece of pottery. It didn't quite happen that way. In reflecting back on the experience, however, I've noticed a remarkable parallel between a potter's work with the clay and a man's relationship with his wife.

A potter begins by centering his clay on the wheel. When the wheel starts turning, he can't just grab the clay. He must carefully but firmly keep the clay in the center of the wheel. He has to work it gently and deliberately, applying just enough pressure to shape it while constantly adding moisture. If he lets the clay get cold, it becomes stiff, resistant, and unworkable. If he neglects the clay and fails to add water, it will dry out and crack. If he stops the process and then starts again, he may force the clay off center, or he may mar it by putting his hands on it too quickly or aggressively. It takes time, but if the potter is patient, creative, and firm but gentle, there's no limit to what he can create.

Do you see the similarities? I am to pursue my wife consistently, warmly, and affectionately, lavishing her with encouragement and affirmation. My approach must be careful and wise, seeking to understand what's going on in Betsy's life and our marriage. Today Betsy may be best served by something out of the blue, a grand stroke of romantic spontaneity. Tomorrow the same approach might completely throw her off center because her need at the moment is to be brought along slowly and gently out of the busyness of life and into the quiet of peaceful intimacy. Every wife is different, and so is every season of life. But like the potter, we are committed to the process as well as to the outcome. And in the end, what was once practiced technique will become a wonderfully creative art form!

Ladies, the analogy may challenge your heart, but shouldn't we long to be clay in our husband's tender grasp? It fits our role as well. We don't want to be unworkable to our husbands. We want to respond to their initiative, always trying to mold toward their leadership. And we don't want to be brittle with expectations either. Perhaps our husbands don't come at this thing of romance naturally. If I resist my husband's attempts at romance because they fail to meet my expectations, I'm setting up the whole process for failure. But if I respond with love and appreciation, he won't be reluctant to try again and will probably do a better job next time. So join in the creative process! What will be your next, unique artistic expression of love for your husband?

Every art has elements that allow the artist to create something beautiful. Music has melody, harmony, and rhythm. Painting has color, texture, and composition. Here are some of the key elements in the art of romance.

### *Creativity*

As much as I (Gary) regularly enjoy giving flowers to Betsy, it must not become predictable. If *every time* I'm out running errands on my day off I "surprise" her by bringing home flowers, well, it's not much of a surprise after a while, is it? Without creativity, romance can easily turn into just another item on the week's agenda. So the question is: What can I do that's new or different or totally random? How can I surprise Betsy with a fresh "I love you"?

I (Betsy) used to feel intimidated by Gary because he is definitely more creative than I am. In my pride I wouldn't launch out for fear of failing. I also saw my own tendency to restrict romance, to put it in a box—candlelit dinners, soft music, and so on. But I've found I can stimulate my creativity by asking other people, "What kinds of things do you do?" With their input I've come to see that romance can include experiencing anything with my husband that I know he enjoys. Sometimes that means stepping outside my comfort zone.

Once while in Norfolk, Virginia, we climbed seventy feet to the top of a nuclear aircraft carrier. You may think, *That's romantic?* But it was delightful. I recall sharing Gary's joy as he sat in the captain's chair, and he still has the photo.

By participating with Gary in things he enjoys, I help forge a lifelong bond of closeness and intimacy between us. I'm not sure I'll ever join him for that flight in an F-14 Tomcat he likes to dream about, but . . .

### *Little Gestures*

Don't underestimate the small things. Holding hands, the way you greet or look at one another, being courteous—simply saying "please," "thank you," and "I love you," respect, kindness, honor—these create an atmosphere of romance. Before we were married, Gary and I were sitting close together in his car (on a bench seat) when an acquaintance leaned in the window and said, "Oh, that's not going to last very long. Seven days after you're married, she's going to be over there and you're going to be over here." Something rose up in me, and I thought, *That will not take place in our marriage!* In the car I still sit as close to Gary as bucket seats will permit (and I, too, miss "The Millennium Falcon"). These little gestures of love help protect a couple from drifting apart.

### *Spontaneous Surprises*

There's nothing quite so romantic as a husband coming home from work and holding up two plane tickets to some exotic destination. But how often can *that* happen? Nevertheless, marriage *can* be filled with spontaneity that is absolutely free.

Gary can be very unpredictable. Now, it would be one thing if we were Fred Astaire and Ginger Rogers, but we're not. So when Gary spontaneously decides to twirl me around in the middle of the mall, part of me would love to be anywhere else at that moment. Yet most of me realizes this is a priceless expression of his love for me.

Then there was dinner at Cinderella's castle in Disney World. He got down on one knee in the middle of the restaurant and presented me a ring to thank me for saying "yes" twenty-seven years ago to the day . . . July 24, 1977. Ah, the joy of living with an adventurous husband. And you know what? I wouldn't change a thing!

## PRIORITIZE ROMANCE AS A WAY OF LIFE

We've already talked a little about the dangers of busyness. Now let's look at some practical steps for making sure "I'm so busy" never becomes "I'm too busy for my spouse," because spontaneity, while a great sign of marital health, is not enough. We also need to *plan* for romance; its priority is reflected in our choices about how we structure our time.

### *Date Nights*

A top priority for any marriage should be consistent date nights out. Of course, getting a regular baby-sitter, if you need one, can be a challenge. During one stretch when we didn't have a consistent date-night baby-sitter, we tried at-home dates. At first they were certainly better than nothing, but eventually I (Betsy) began using the time to catch up on housework. Pretty soon date night became catch-up night. Slowly housework began to seem more important to me than romance. Talk about misplaced priorities!

This prompts me (Gary) to stress how important it is for the husband to take the leadership and initiative in pursuing romance. It should begin with taking responsibility for date-night baby-sitters if you need them. What a romantic gesture to our wives! What a way to show our interest in being alone with them—by personally arranging for a baby-sitter.

Another way to take initiative is to set the agenda for dates. "So, like, whaddya wanna do tonight?" is not good leadership. Nor is asking her for three ideas and picking the one you like best. Feel free to get her preferences, but make sure you determine the plan and then take action. Guess what? You'll have a far more enjoyable evening leading through an idea that didn't go quite as planned than not leading through an idea that wasn't planned at all!

I recommend, if possible, one evening together each week alone and away from home. This may seem like a luxury—an ideal, perhaps, but not very realistic. If that's how you view it, we'd like to challenge you to reconsider. Every couple serious about deepening their intimacy needs to have regular time when they can anticipate being together apart from the distractions of the home, job, responsibilities, and, if applicable, the children.

Your finances may lead you to think a weekly date is impossible, but your time together doesn't have to be expensive to be enjoyable. Instead of dinner, take a walk in the park or a drive in the country. Share an ice cream sundae or pack your own picnic. Ask your friends for ideas. Scan your local newspaper for possible activities. To minimize baby-sitting costs, look for another couple willing to swap child care with you on a regular basis. If you're creative and resourceful and romance is a priority, finances will never keep you from enjoying weekly time together.

### *Weekend Getaways*

Spending concentrated time with each other in a different environment is an excellent way to refresh and refocus your marriage. Betsy and I once read an article suggesting that every couple should have a special getaway location. While you don't want to get in a vacation rut, it's great to have a place you can find without getting lost, where you know what to expect—a place that becomes familiar through repeated visits and memories. Ours is Colonial Williamsburg. It's a standard joke among our friends that if Betsy and I go out of town, we must be in Williamsburg.

### *Celebrations and Traditions*

Birthdays and holidays, milestones and anniversaries (whether serious or silly) offer a gold mine of romantic opportunity. Celebration punctuates the daily routine with life and color.

Gary and I used to mark the anniversary of our engagement by going to the restaurant where he proposed to me. We'd make reservations for the same time and the same table—the one in the corner with the little hole in the window.

Because we were married in mid-October, we developed a tradition of going away for our wedding anniversary and beginning our Christmas shopping together.

Every year we watch the 1939 film version of *A Christmas Carol*. Early in our marriage (before videos and DVDs) we realized one year that it was nowhere to be found on TV. I (Gary) discovered that the library had it on 16mm film. So I checked out the film and a projector, picked up some popcorn, and, accompanied by the soft clicking of projector reels, Betsy and I were able to snuggle through a delightful tradition preserved!

I (Betsy) never know what to expect on Valentine's Day! One year I woke up in the middle of the night, in labor with our fourth child. Gary wasn't in bed, so I went downstairs . . . and caught him in the act. He was covering the entire front of the house in bright red plastic tablecloths on which were bold white letters announcing, "Gary Loves Betsy." The next day he added, "It's a Boy!" You can probably imagine how the neighbors reacted to his less-than-subtle display of love and affection. For a while all Gary got from the men was, "Thanks a lot!"

### *Resources for Romance*

When we moved to our current neighborhood, I (Gary) made a point of finding out where the florists were. Today the research is easier; most grocery stores contain a reasonably priced flower shop.

Be sure you know your spouse's favorites—candy, music, clothes, books, etc.—and where to get them. Stock up on greeting cards so you're prepared for any occasion (after a conflict, on your way out the door in the morning, after making love).

Always be looking for new ways and times to communicate, "I appreciate who you are and who you are to me." When giving your spouse a card or note, make finding it as much of an adventure as reading it. Place it in the freezer, dryer, cereal box, pillow case, or medicine cabinet. Tape one to the steering wheel, or have the children deliver it (but don't expect them to keep a secret very well).

### *Gifts*

If giving your spouse a new food processor or leaf rake is your idea of romance, you're to be commended for reading this far! Practical items like those should be given only if seriously needed or requested. Romantic gifts should appeal more to your spouse's interests than to his or her needs. What does your spouse enjoy? What are the things he or she gravitates to in terms of hobbies, interests, and spare time?

Betsy enjoys receiving books as well as flowers and perfume. She also likes getting clothes. The selection of styles and fashions can seem overwhelming, but I've made a point of remembering her clothing sizes and favorite colors.

### *Photographs*

Keep a picture of your spouse in your office and in your wallet or purse—anyplace where you will look at it frequently. Put pictures of you together on your computer desktop. This says something to your spouse and to the people around you about your values and priorities. A couple of years ago Gary had his picture taken for a brochure that the church was producing. When I saw the finished product, there was Gary, seated in his office, with a picture of me and the children behind him. He had rearranged his desk to be sure that picture of us was included in the photo. It meant so much to me that he thought about including us and then made the effort to do so.

### *Wish Lists*

Learn all you can about your spouse by studying his or her interests. What things would he or she take delight in? What would be meaningful? Gary's interests cover the spectrum—from watercolor painting to Abraham Lincoln to Walt Disney to naval aviation and everything in between. To help me know him better, I've asked him to put together a wish list of the things, big or little, he would enjoy. Now, chances are I will never give Gary a watercolor painting of Abe Lincoln and Mickey Mouse in the cockpit of a fighter jet, but I can keep my eyes open at the mall for something he loves that just might be on sale. It's a joy for me simply to know what would delight Gary. His wish list is a great source of ideas for how I can please him.

Guys, study your wife. What does she enjoy for recreation, leisure, or cultural entertainment? Where does she like to go for walks? What does she like to read? What are her favorite desserts, refreshments, and restaurants? What kind of music does she like? Each of these can provide you with one more way to surprise and delight your bride, the wife of your youth, the love of your life.

### *Pet Names*

Pet names add a playful and intimate quality to your relationship. These are affectionate terms you use only with your spouse, out of earshot (hopefully) of everyone else.

Twice a year the pastors of Covenant Life Church get away together for four days of worship, prayer, study, and fellowship. On one of these retreats, before the days of cell phones, I (Gary) was on the phone with Betsy, trying to address her discreetly by one of our favorite pet names. Now, my closest friends are these men on our pastoral team. There are no men I respect more and no one, except my family, with whom I share more of my personal life. But even this has its limits, and at that moment I didn't realize one of the guys could hear me.

I soon learned there are no secrets among friends.

To this day, if the pastors are having a meeting and I have to step out of the room, someone might still blurt out, "So, going to go call ________, are you?" (Sorry, having these guys know is bad enough.)

### *Lasting Memories*

One final suggestion: Have some way of recording the memories you make as husband and wife. Once you've invested the time and money to do something special, invest just a little extra effort to preserve it. Take photos. Shoot a video. Create a photo album devoted to romantic memories you've made. As one example, we have a large montage of honeymoon memorabilia on our rec room wall.

## SO HOW DO WE GET STARTED?

We've covered so many ideas in this chapter that it would be easy to feel overwhelmed. Perhaps you're thinking, *How am I possibly going to do all this?* You can't . . . at least, not all at once.

A lifestyle of romance can't be developed overnight, but it can be begun. Start with your heart. Is romance a priority? If not, what has to change?

Next, pick just one thing in this chapter and do it. Immediately—as in right now (if you can) . . . today (if at all possible) . . . tomorrow, *at the absolute latest*. This is your marriage we're talking about! Your wife is your best friend, your lover! In God's eyes there is nothing in your life more important than loving God and loving your spouse.

After you do that one thing, try another! The key is to start somewhere and slowly develop consistency. Don't get discouraged if something goes awry. That can be a delightful memory as well.

Men, God has given us primary responsibility for leadership in pursuing romance. Even if it seems artificial or awkward, we need to begin implementing the kinds of ideas presented in this chapter. Romantic actions will lead to romantic feelings. Don't waste time. Get started. And, ladies, please be receptive to any initiative your husband may take. It's fine if he borrows ideas directly from this book—that's one reason we've written it! Be patient and encourage him as he takes whatever steps he is able to take right now, even if they are small.

Also, men, be very careful not to place any expectations on your wife's response. If romance has not been your strong suit, don't expect an overwhelming expression of gratitude and admiration from her. That may not happen the first time. Or the second. Or the third. But as long as you are faithful and continue to communicate your love through sincere attempts at romance, God will help her respond in time.

Let me (Betsy) interject here. Ladies, we shouldn't just sit around waiting for our husbands to shower us with romance. We have a responsibility as well to take initiative and show creativity. By doing our part, we make it easier for our husbands to do theirs.

You've probably guessed this by now, but when Betsy and I think of romance, we don't think first in terms of champagne, exotic vacations, dozens of roses, or expensive gifts. Romance to us simply means communicating—in as many consistent and creative ways as we can—that our spouse is the most important, precious, desirable person we will ever know. That's what we want in our marriage. On occasion we will do something lavish, but the heart of our relationship consists of spending time together, sharing favorites and memories, laughing, crying, doing goofy things together, or quietly talking over iced tea out on the deck. That's intimate friendship. That's becoming one. That's romance.

God's ultimate purpose for romance is the same as his purpose for marriage: to bring himself glory, to bring us blessing, and to demonstrate the remarkable relationship between Christ and the Church. Merely being faithful to your spouse is quite a testimony in the twenty-first century. But as you go beyond that to communicate passionate love for your spouse in consistent, creative, uninhibited ways, whether by a tender caress or a ten-day cruise, the world can't help but notice. God will be wonderfully honored, and you will be building into your marriage a romance that never has to get old, a passion that will last from the next time you say "I love you" to the last time you whisper "Good-bye."

A favorite and frequent exchange between Betsy and me for twenty-eight years now, referring to our engagement and marriage, goes like this: "Love, thanks for saying 'yes.'" To which Betsy softly smiles and simply says, "Thanks for asking."

How can you begin today to creatively tell your spouse, "I love you, and I'm so very glad you're mine"?

8

# Just the Two of You

## THE WONDER OF SEXUAL INTIMACY

Sex—or more accurately, distortions, perversions, idealized imagery, and unreliable or unhelpful information *about* sex—is everywhere. It's on TV, in the movies, in malls, in music, lurking on the Internet, and staring at you from the front pages of the grocery-line tabloids.

Now, marriage is the one place you might imagine people could talk freely about sex. How sad then that there's probably no area in marriage that occupies more of our thought but less of our talk than the sexual relationship! We think about it, worry about it, or dream about it. Yet most couples spend very little time actually discussing how they can achieve greater sexual intimacy, sexual joy, and sexual satisfaction. This is so unfortunate. How often have you found yourself thinking along these lines:

*I wonder if he has any idea what I long for in our sexual relationship?*

*Does she know what really brings me physical satisfaction?*

*Wouldn't it be nice to talk as openly about lovemaking as we do about our budget or our schedule?*

It's no surprise that questions like these rarely come out in the open. Fear, guilt, comparison, and pride all war against humble questions, requests, and conversation. We trust, however, that this chapter will encourage candid and consistent conversation between you and your spouse as you work toward a truly and mutually fulfilling sexual relationship.

If curiosity has led you to look at this chapter first, you should realize that we have placed it at the end of the book for a good reason. Your enjoyment of physical intimacy won't be complete until you've cultivated spiritual and emotional intimacy—the focus of the first seven chapters. C.J. Mahaney expresses it clearly when he writes:

> In a strong Christian marriage that glorifies God, a couple's enjoyment of one another takes place on a long continuum of romantic affection and expression. It's a continuum made up of many points. Toward one end are things like "companionship" and "fellowship." Toward the other end are things like "playful intimacy" and "really serious sex." But exactly where one point on the continuum begins and the other ends isn't always clear. That's because solid Christian marriages are not primarily about one point or another. They're about the entire continuum—the relationship itself.[27]

So please don't try to separate sex from the rest of your marriage. It is neither an afterthought nor the starting point. Satisfying sex is vitally linked to every other topic covered in this book.

## Sexual Intimacy and God

Any fruitful and accurate discussion of sexuality must begin with our Creator. Sex didn't originate with sin. God commanded Adam and Eve to "be fruitful and multiply" before anyone ever touched the forbidden fruit (Genesis 1:28). Sex within marriage, with all its unifying pleasure and procreative power, was God's idea, not ours. He is the author of our sexuality. When we develop a satisfying sexual relationship with our spouse, we honor God as the Creator and designer of sex.

The Bible speaks very openly and frankly about sex in marriage. In Proverbs 5:15-19, for example, husbands are given an explicit picture of sexual passion and intimacy and are commanded to "rejoice in the wife of your youth." The Song of Songs, as we saw in Chapter Seven, is an entire book of Scripture celebrating the goodness and wonder of marital love and sexual intimacy in marriage. When Paul told Corinthian couples not to "deprive one another" (1 Corinthians 7:2-5), it's quite clear he was referring to the pleasure and joy of sexual activity. Invariably, the Bible describes sex within the covenant of marriage as delightful, pleasurable, and sacred (e.g., Song 4:16—5:1). Our view should be no less positive.

Some translations of the Bible, including the King James Version and the English Standard Version, often refer to the sexual act as a man "knowing" his wife. This implies a rich, experiential union, something sacred and intensely personal. Any man and woman can have intercourse. But to make love with one's spouse, to know him or her in this deepest possible way, is an experience found only in the covenant of marriage.

It's amazing how many Christians are either surprised to discover or reluctant to admit that God designed us for sexual pleasure as well as for procreation. Some are simply ignorant of how the Bible presents marital intimacy. Others struggle with the personal disappointment and shame of their own sexual past. But God is gracious and redemptive, and despite all the misrepresentations, misunderstandings, and sinful distortions, physical intimacy within marriage can be a biblical, beautiful, and enjoyable gift from God. And like all of God's gifts, the sexual relationship of a husband and wife is meant to get better with time.

If the sexual relationship in your marriage is healthy and strong, this chapter will help you keep it that way, and hopefully even improve it. But maybe it isn't; it's neither healthy nor strong. Misinformation, negative experiences, and unbiblical attitudes can decimate the joyful sexuality that God intends for every marriage. But know this: based on almost thirty years of counseling couples, trust us when we say you are not alone.

Sexual problems in marriage, even fairly serious problems, are not uncommon. Some couples, when they understand biblical truth about sex in marriage and learn to talk openly with one another, can emerge rather easily from sexual difficulties. Other couples' problems may take a lot of hard work to understand and address. But the hope offered to each marriage is the same: God intends sexuality to be a rich blessing to you, and that blessing is received by understanding biblical truth, and then speaking freely with one another about your sexual relationship.

We ought to be able to share all our fears, experiences, and desires with one another in marriage. But what so often happens is that sexual frustration, disappointment, or unmet expectations lead to decreased physical involvement . . . and silence. Rather than opening up and discussing what's wrong, the unfulfilled spouse backs away. Sometimes he or she actually comes to see sex as distasteful or simply unnecessary. That's why one goal of this chapter is to get you and your spouse talking about sex in constructive, biblical ways.

It all begins with a scriptural understanding of sexuality. Once we have stopped reducing or rejecting God's Word because it doesn't line up with our experience, our experience can begin to be brought up to the level of Scripture. As you patiently and diligently work toward change, relying on the grace and wisdom of God, you and your spouse will replace worldly attitudes with biblical attitudes, create fruitful experiences in place of disappointing experiences, and renew your minds regarding God's plan for the physical relationship.

I (Gary) have written the next portion of this chapter specifically for husbands. After that, Betsy will address wives. Though we encourage both of you to read the chapter in its entirety, focus on what God is saying to *you*—not what he may or may not be saying to your spouse.

Before we continue, we must again offer thanks and recognition to two of our closest friends, C.J. and Carolyn Mahaney. Over the years their instruction, counsel, and example have informed just about every area of our lives, marriage, and family. By God's grace we incorporated their wisdom into our ministry as well as into our relationship. So as we prepared outlines, messages, and seminars, we adapted and included much of what we had been taught.

Recently, C.J. and Carolyn served us all by taking their wealth of wisdom and experience and condensing it onto two outstanding books, *Sex, Romance, and the Glory of God* by C.J. and *Feminine Appeal* by Carolyn. Parts of this book, especially this chapter, owe much to the Mahaneys' prior investment. So let what you find in these next pages be an introduction to the fuller treatment you will find in those volumes . . . which you must read!

So many couples could enjoy a far more satisfying sexual relationship if they would simply learn to discuss the subject. And as you will see, from those books and from this chapter, there is plenty to talk about.

## Sexuality and the Husband

Gentlemen, none of us was born with a gift for lovemaking. We were born with a sinful predisposition to selfishness! The mentality that "it all comes naturally" is a delusion and a major hindrance to the development of our sexual experience. And all that "instruction" we picked up in locker rooms, movies, magazines, or the Internet? The vast majority was lies, doing infinitely more harm than good. Consequently, many of us find we've been married for years and don't really know what we're doing . . . and now we're too proud or fearful to admit it.

So in order for a man to develop a sexual relationship that truly satisfies his wife and himself and brings God's grace to their union, he must start with humility and an eagerness to learn—a process of discovery that will last years beyond the wedding night.

Do you find yourself frustrated or confused by some aspect of your sexual relationship? That's a perfect opportunity to humble yourself and ask for help. If pride is keeping you from seeking advice from others, then your lack of progress may in part indicate that God is resisting you, for he opposes the proud but gives grace to the humble (James 4:6; 1 Peter 5:5). We cannot build a successful marriage without help from others, starting with our wives. Men, we must not let embarrassment (often a euphemism for pride and fear) keep us from the will and purpose of God.

What hinders us in our pursuit of a satisfying sexual relationship? What keeps us from taking steps toward the openness and intimacy we long for?

• Is there a fear of talking about sex with our wives or with others, whether with other men or as couples?

• Are we tempted to judge our wives in terms of how we assume they will respond when we initiate the conversation?

• Do we believe the lie that sexual problems or difficulties are abnormal? This is a lie that survives on silence. If we were open enough to discuss our experiences with others, we'd find that almost every man has faced similar situations.

• Are we hindered by pride, fear, or shame about our skill as lovers? Who would want to admit, for example, that he has difficulty maintaining an erection? Guys, the grace for help is usually only a humble conversation away.

• Finally, do we need to be delivered from the arrogance that deceives us into believing we know it all? It's far less risky to just ask your wife what feels good than to assume and stumble into a memorable catastrophe.

Once you can admit you are still learning, then do the obvious: learn! As Dr. Ed Wheat writes in his uniquely helpful and practical book *Intended for Pleasure*, "Please note that this is a *learning* process, with husband and wife progressively discovering how to provide pleasure for each other. They begin with some explicit information (the more the better); then with growing delight, they find out by experience and application of information just how to make love and impart maximum joy to their mate."[28] So commit yourself to study, search the Scriptures, read the books recommended at the end of this book, and ask questions of mature and trusted friends. Most importantly, talk to your wife about your sex life! Ask her questions. Share your thoughts, dreams, desires, and any fears.

Our sexual awareness depends not only on communication that takes place in the bedroom but on what and how we have communicated in other ways throughout the day. Lovemaking is infinitely more than a technique: it's a relationship. Once again Dr. Wheat provides wisdom and insight:

> Sexual intercourse can be a joyful affirmation of the life two people share, or it can be a revelation of defects in their relationship. It will either draw a couple together or push them apart. Because your sexual relationship will tend to reflect your emotional relationship, it is important to realize that every meaningful, fully enjoyable sex act really begins with a loving, attentive attitude hours or even days before. Husband, you should be aware that your wife views the sex act as part of her total relationship with you, even though you, like other

> men, may think of it separately. When both partners assume the responsibility for giving of their total selves—physically, emotionally, and spiritually—sexual interaction becomes a dynamic way of fully expressing love for each other. *It is your daily behavior toward each other* that will measure the extent and depth of the pleasure you find in making love sexually.[29]

Sexual proficiency will also require practice, practice, practice. In order to improve, you're going to have to spend some time making love to your wife. (This has got to be the best homework assignment you've ever been given.) Just make sure your motive is to learn and improve and please your wife so you can consistently serve her with at least the same diligence with which you seek to satisfy your own sexual desires. Skillful and sensitive lovemaking for the pleasure of our spouse is an art we're to develop for the rest of our lives.

### *Your Wife's Sexuality*

Here's a statement you may want to post on the headboard of your bed: *My wife is aroused differently than I am. She is much more complex than I am, both physically and emotionally. It's not enough for me to stimulate her body. She needs my tender acceptance. She needs my understanding. And she needs to know that I cherish and honor her, especially in my sexual desires and pursuit.* You can add this P.S. from C.J. Mahaney who wisely advises, "In order for romance to deepen, you must touch the heart and mind of your wife before you touch her body."[30]

Women are stimulated by *inward emotions* as well as by *gentle and affectionate physical contact.* As a rule, men are sexually stimulated by what they *see.* The following bedtime scenario illustrates the difference. You're in bed reading an interesting and inspiring biography when your wife enters the room. As she begins to undress, you find yourself rather distracted and your reading drifting . . . drifting. Within seconds you have forgotten what page you were on, and even what book you were reading. As she slips under the covers you're interested all right, but that book isn't even on the radar screen.

Hopping out of bed the next morning, you step on the book, still lying where it fell, and smile.

Now if the tables are turned and it's the wife who is reading in bed, sometimes she will respond to visual stimulation. But many times she will just continue to read until you begin to pursue her tenderly and affectionately. Don't take it personally, guys. Women are just different than we are!

Speaking of differences . . . we interrupt this program to bring you a refresher in female anatomy.

For most of us, eighth-grade biology was a long time ago in a galaxy far, far away! And since you probably won't visit a bookstore between now and the next time you and your wife make love, let's revisit a few of the particulars here.

Most men think that simply entering the vagina touches the woman's center of sexuality and pleasure. It doesn't. This may be the source of *your* greatest pleasure, but not necessarily hers. That's why actual intercourse, if begun prematurely, may be very satisfying to the man but not to the woman.

The most keenly sensitive part of a woman's anatomy is the clitoris. This has been called the trigger of female desire. What function does the clitoris serve? Apparently none other than to facilitate sexual arousal and pleasure. This gives the phrase "fearfully and wonderfully made" (Psalm 139:14) a whole new significance! During lovemaking the clitoris must be stimulated either directly or indirectly for the wife to achieve orgasm.

We now return to our regularly scheduled program.

The admonition to "live with your wives in an understanding way" (1 Peter 3:7) has tremendous application and relevance when we're talking about sexuality. How well do you understand your wife's sexual makeup? What gives her pleasure? What does she find uncomfortable? What stirs her desire? What hinders her desire?

Each of us needs to become skillful in enhancing our wife's enjoyment. Don't assume you know what she likes, and don't limit the areas available for sexual exploration. If you always make love the same way, your routine will lead to boredom, and boredom will lead you right out of the bedroom. Discover what pleases her and when. Look for new ways to delight her. Keep in mind that her responses may vary. What brought passion and pleasure on Monday may bring only giggles of playfulness on Thursday. Don't try to figure it out. Just laugh along with her.

### *Motive, Understanding, and Timing*

A heart to serve genuinely and sacrificially is a prerequisite for success in marriage. Sexual intimacy and satisfaction must begin with giving—giving not only your body for the pleasure of your spouse, but also giving your understanding, patience, and sensitivity. Do not make demands.

As a man, your sexual appetite may reflect a physiological desire, as well as a desire for relational intimacy. That physiological desire should be openly and humbly expressed, but don't let it control your behavior. You must be aware of your wife's emotional and physical readiness. Where is she in her menstrual cycle? How demanding has the day been for her? If she is ill or in some other way limited in her ability to engage sexually, consider with her any creative alternatives to intercourse, or perhaps postpone your time of intimacy. Don't become resentful or bitter, and don't project guilt. Unless there's a pattern of refusal, an occasional delay in order to serve your wife won't hurt you. (It may require some self-control, but it won't do any permanent damage.)

If you feel a pattern of sexual refusal is emerging, share your questions, concerns, and experiences with your wife *without accusing her*. Perhaps your wife is unaware or for some reason reluctant. If your discussions aren't fruitful or mutually satisfying, or if a long-term problem or impasse develops, talk to your pastor or a mature couple. Get help. This kind of situation never just goes away.

### *Anticipation and Preparation*

Remember, the sexual experience begins well before you reach the bedroom. I strongly recommend you reread parts of the chapter on romance. (I know I need to be reminded once in a while!) Have you built anticipation for sexual intimacy and pleasure with your words, kindness, and affection? Have you emotionally prepared for time together? That's not to say there won't be situations when you're close together in the kitchen, look into one another's eyes, and quickly decide, "The dishes can wait!" But in either case, how you conduct the journey is obviously vital to arriving at the desired destination.

As a rule, but not always, our wives tend to arouse more slowly and gradually than we do. Their sexual desire has emotional, relational, and spiritual dimensions in addition to the physical. And if their emotions are affected by other things, no amount of contact is going to bring them to a place of arousal. Learn to appreciate this aspect of your wife's sexuality. Her marvelously complex patterns of arousal simply indicate she is different, not deficient.

How can a man gently and patiently lead his wife into lovemaking? (Men, this can build anticipation for us and add to the pleasure of our own experience, if we let it.) Begin by creating an atmosphere of total, undistracted privacy. Make sure the shades are drawn, the doors are locked, and any children are asleep or *completely* distracted. If you've ever heard that little knock at the door indicating that the Winnie the Pooh video was not quite as long as you thought, I know you understand.

Our children are now twenty-three (and just married!), twenty-one, nineteen, and fourteen. They all had "the talk" years ago and are often awake much later than we are. Three of them sleep in bedrooms next to or across the hall from ours! Talk about the need for creativity and planning or for spontaneously seizing the moment! In fact, at this point I'm pretty sure they realize that "Dad and Mom need to talk" is simply code for "Do Not Disturb," and they're just being gracious about it.

Once you've established privacy, set an atmosphere of romance, relaxation, and anticipation. Candlelight and soft music are almost always good for this. Avoid discussing topics that could distract your wife. In other words, this isn't the best time to talk about buying a new car or whom to invite to the Super Bowl party. If you're planning to spend time together sexually, consider a fresh shower and shave. Of course there may be—and should be—spontaneous times of lovemaking when many of these preliminaries are happily thrown out the window. As long as the desire is mutual, "Quick Encounters of a Close Kind" can definitely add a spirit of adventure to your sexual relationship.

### *Foreplay and Intercourse*

As you're preparing for intimacy, talk to your wife and determine her mood so you know how to approach her. Sometimes she may be excited by your being strongly aggressive. At other times she may desire an approach that's more prolonged, gentle, and tender. Encourage her to direct your caresses and contact in ways that please her. It's not your job as a leader to know automatically what she wants. You're supposed to find out, and the best way to find out is to ask. As a couple, you should increasingly feel the freedom to discuss your sexual desires as they unfold during lovemaking.

On the other hand, if she seems to be thoroughly enjoying the experience, a game of Twenty Questions may only be a distraction. So how will you know? Just like everybody else—through the humbling process of experience.

In general, the husband begins and finishes every phase of lovemaking more quickly than his wife. If he selfishly runs ahead at his own pace, she will be left behind, if not left out altogether. It's imperative that the husband look beyond his own gratification and strive to serve and please his wife. In the marriage bed, the choice between servanthood and selfishness may determine whether your wife feels cherished or used. Think about it.

More often than not, you and your wife will need time to build up to maximum sexual fulfillment. This is the purpose of foreplay. During this stage of intimacy the man must be patient, tender, and skillful. Many of the problems in our sexual relationship begin here. We simply forget how different our wives are in this respect. The wife likes to be wooed and won. The husband likes . . . well, we already know what the husband likes.

A woman finds sexual intimacy most satisfying when it takes place in a context of intimate sharing, communication, and affection. Those take time. But making love to your wife verbally is as important as making love to her physically. Remember, touch her heart and mind before you touch her body. Besides, a creative approach to foreplay helps keep your sexual involvement from becoming mechanical. Also, recognize that your wife can't speed up her responses or her different phases of arousal. Not that she's any less sensual—it just takes her body a little longer to go from 0 to 60 mph. We must be patient and loving, making sure our time together is an event and not just an act.

Begin your time of lovemaking with gentle affection and contact: kissing, embracing, caressing, fondling, exploring. Don't be afraid to try different positions. There should be a total freedom to give yourselves to one another in any way that is pleasurable, as long as it is not offensive to your partner. Continue to communicate clearly as your feelings intensify.

Timing the transition to intercourse—that wondrous phase in which the two of you become one flesh—is crucial. The only way you'll know you're both ready is to communicate with each other. Though perhaps awkward at first, communication gets easier and easier with practice. Not only does it make for a smooth transition, but it enhances the act of intercourse.

You were both created to experience orgasm or climax. Although this doesn't always happen, that doesn't necessarily mean anything is wrong. Remarkably (at least, it seems remarkable to guys), at times a woman can find intercourse wonderfully pleasurable and satisfying even without an orgasm, because for her this is a total relational experience—and that's fine, as long as both of you are pursuing the maximum pleasure and satisfaction for the other, and not yielding to resignation, reluctance, or neglect. Almost as remarkably, a woman can have varying levels or degrees of ecstasy in her orgasm. She is even capable of multiple orgasms as her clitoris is gently and continually stimulated. (That, by the way, is something for scientific research! Perhaps I'm just missing something, but I have found that my allotment is one!)

Premature ejaculation may bring your lovemaking to an end before your wife has reached climax. This is a fairly common problem for men. Talk about it. Get counsel from your pastor or perhaps your doctor. It will take some time, effort, and more than a little humility, but you'll have been faithful to pursue your wife's greatest enjoyment and satisfaction.

Once intercourse culminates in orgasm, you may be ready to move on to other things (sleeping, for example). But recognize that women often take longer for their experience of ecstasy and sensitivity to subside. Don't be in a hurry to draw apart. Continue to lie close to your wife, holding her in your arms as you express your gratitude and appreciation for her. Encourage her skill as a lover. Use this time simply to enjoy one another. These moments of lingering together in the afterglow of lovemaking can be as rewarding and fulfilling as any other part of your experience.

## Sexuality and the Wife

Again, with much gratefulness to Carolyn Mahaney, one of my closest friends, let me (Betsy) begin this section for wives by saying as forcefully as I know how that sex is a gift from God to be thoroughly enjoyed by both husband and wife within the boundaries of marriage.

A gift? Yes! To be enjoyed? Thoroughly! God created us to have body parts that when touched bring great delight and pleasure. If God had not intended for women to enjoy physical intimacy, he could have easily designed us differently.

Our sexual relationship is to be an oasis in marriage. Some of you may think, *An oasis? Not quite. To me sex is a chore, a duty, just one more need I'm expected to meet.* Or perhaps you want it to be an oasis, but your husband seems disinterested. He doesn't pursue you. Well, what then? The first step to solving problems or difficulties in our lives is to discover what God's will is for our situation. God's Word offers insights that can liberate every wife to fully enjoy her sexual relationship with her husband.

At the same time, let's cultivate realistic expectations. We can't hope to attain a consistently blissful sexual relationship overnight. It is a learned experience. For many of us, the learning process will take a lot of patience, work, effort, and even some tears and pain. But when we know God's intent for our sexual relationship with our husbands, we can be sure that God will help us and change us. Carolyn Mahaney writes:

> Marital sex is the pinnacle of human bonding. It is the highest form of the communication of love—a language that expresses love without words. It calls forth the deepest, most powerful emotions. It creates intimacy within marriage like nothing else. In fact, as we give and receive the gift of lovemaking, this intimacy will grow stronger and more precious as the years go by. Each encounter will lead us to a deeper "knowing" of the one we love.[31]

It's tragic that so many couples are either unaware of their need for help or are unwilling to ask for it. Sexual problems generate incredible levels of anxiety, apprehension, frustration, and guilt. They also expose pride and fear, thus hindering couples from seeking the help they so desperately need. But the fact is, when you bring two adults together who have different desires, personalities, and backgrounds, it would be highly unusual for them not to have some sexual adjustments or difficulties.

It may take a long time to work through the more challenging aspects of your sexual relationship, but don't let sin hinder you or Satan condemn you. God wants to change you, encourage you, liberate you, and help you to experience all he intends for you. Ask for his help.

My approach to this material will be a little different from Gary's, but I believe it provides a biblical standard for relating to our husbands sexually. Join me as we consider eight characteristics of a creative lover.

### *She Is Available*

Imagine yourself at 11:00 P.M., collapsing on the bed after an exhausting day. Then you notice that look in your husband's eye and realize he's not thinking about sleep—at least not yet. Inwardly you groan and think to yourself, *Can't he see I'm exhausted? He has no idea how draining my day was*. At that moment it may seem perfectly legitimate to postpone intimacy by appealing to your fatigue. But Scripture must be the final word on this:

> *The husband should give to his wife her conjugal rights, and likewise the wife to her husband. For the wife does not have authority over her own body, but the husband does. Likewise the husband does not have authority over his own body, but the wife does. Do not deprive one another, except perhaps by agreement for a limited time, that you may devote yourselves to prayer; but then come together again, so that Satan may not tempt you because of your lack of self-control.* (1 Corinthians 7:3-5)

There are three clear and inescapable points in this passage. 1) In matters of sexuality, the spouse's body belongs to the other. 2) Therefore, denying sex to one another is never legitimate. 3) In fact, abstaining from sex should only take place when three conditions are met: you both agree to it, the abstention is temporary, and it's intended to serve a season in which prayer is particularly emphasized.

That's right: satisfying your husband's sexual desires—and he satisfying yours—is so important that prayer is the only legitimate reason for abstaining if there is no actual physical hindrance. And even that needs to be by mutual consent.

Ladies, when your husband initiates lovemaking, what's on the line is nothing less than his heart, his leadership, and his perception of your respect for him. Consistent refusal and rejection could tempt him in ways you might never imagine! Remember this the next time you're "not in the mood." Instead of looking at your own circumstances, look to God's Word and cry out for the grace to serve your husband.

A few simple changes in your lifestyle might make a big difference in helping you not to deprive your husband. If you're tired and you know your husband wants to make love, try taking a shower to wake up. A nap in the middle of the day (if possible) will put you in a much better mood for intimacy at night. Or how about waking up extra early? This has been one of our most effective solutions.

Because Gary and I have three children at home and full schedules, we've found it essential to schedule times of intimacy together. That may not sound very romantic, but it helps me prepare myself emotionally to make the most of those times. For many women the struggle to serve their husbands is more emotional than physical: they lack desire for physical intimacy. My response is simple: right action generates genuine desire! If you are faithful to give yourself (and give yourself in faith) to your husband, I guarantee you the desire and pleasure will come back, because God wants to bless your marriage and will always bless humility and faith.

At the other end of the spectrum are women eager for sexual intimacy, but their husbands show little interest or initiative. That can tempt and hurt very deeply. All I can offer is this simple, four-step approach:

- Bathe your concerns in prayer.
- Prepare your thoughts carefully.
- Ask the Lord to keep your heart right.
- Then *lovingly* appeal to your husband.

If the problem continues, get help from a mature and trusted couple. But while you pursue and appeal, don't resort to disrespect or bitterness—your sin will only make matters worse. Once you have explained to your husband your desires and motives and have asked for his help, turn your husband over to the Holy Spirit. God will meet your needs.

I don't make that last statement flippantly. Trusting God may be the hardest thing we've ever done, but that's what we need to do because without faith toward God we cannot please him.

An atmosphere of total availability acts as a safeguard for our marriages. Our husbands are continually bombarded by sexual temptation via the newspaper, TV, magazines, billboards, the Internet, and the women's fashion industry. And though men may be more vulnerable to this, you and I are far from immune. If you find yourself fantasizing about other men or in any other way violating your covenant with your husband, consider how frequently you are having sexual relations with your husband. Increased time with your husband will decrease his temptation—and yours—to look elsewhere.

### *She Is Carefree*

Men can often be aroused regardless of their emotions, but a woman is not that way. Her sexual response is closely tied to her emotional state. If she's experiencing anxiety, thinking of all the unfinished projects around the house, or feeling bitter about something her husband said or did, these will negatively affect her participation in physical intimacy. You will not be able to make love freely if you're thinking about what to serve for dinner or worrying that the kids are finger-painting the kitchen table. I don't know of any magical formulas for removing these feelings. You must simply purpose to set those anxieties aside and concentrate on your husband.

On occasion I find myself in the middle of a very full day or preoccupied with some concern and my husband will start to pursue me. Inside I'm thinking, *Oh no, how can I make a transition here?* Over the years I've become much more flexible (and believe me, it has taken years!). I've realized that in most cases, everything I need to get done will get done, even if it has to wait a bit. At other times, if my mind is racing, Gary and I will lie close for a while with quiet conversation and gentle caresses. This does wonders for unburdening my mind and gets it racing in a more exciting direction!

### *She Is Attractive*

Before I was married, I never left the house looking bad . . . but you should have seen me in the house! I didn't bother freshening up, wearing makeup, or fixing my hair. And I'm afraid I took those habits with me into marriage. It took a close friend's example and encouragement to help me change. If I want my husband to desire me, I need to look desirable. These things have become important to me because I want to treat Gary with real respect.

Women often pay less attention to their appearance after they get married. Yet our appearance is more important now than ever. Most of our husbands work in an environment where they are surrounded by women striving to look attractive. We need to look attractive when they leave for work and when they come home. Attractive undergarments and nightwear are also important. It takes effort to look good, especially if you have small children. There will inevitably be those crazy days when you barely get out of your robe. But on the whole we need to attend to our appearance. This is a tangible and meaningful way to express love and respect for our husbands.

### *She Is Eager*

Few things will bless our husbands more than knowing we look forward to our sexual experiences with them. Have you ever communicated to your husband that you can't wait to make love with him again? Try it! It will encourage him and enhance your anticipation at the same time. And if your eagerness needs a boost, recall your last pleasurable and passionate experience. What led up to it? What did you most enjoy about it? Let your fond recollection stir your own desire to give and to receive pleasure. Now, where can you begin?

### *She Is Creative*

Study your husband. What excites him? What draws him to you? What pleases him? Not all men are alike. There will always be new discoveries to make as your relationship grows. Find out what uniquely appeals to him, and then pursue creative ways to light the flames of passion.

I am not by nature a creative person, but I've found creativity can be learned! Ask your husband about his desires and dreams for your sexual relationship and then put those into action. Learn from other creative friends, and adapt their ideas to your own sexual relationship.

### *She Is Adventurous*

We should each make it our goal to assure that lovemaking never becomes a predictable or boring experience. Although the definition of adventure will differ from couple to couple, let me ask you some questions so you can assess how adventurous you are:

- Are you willing to make love at unorthodox times?
- Are you willing to try new places (as long as they are private)?
- Are you willing to try new things?

I find the second question to be the most challenging of the three. But I must be willing to try! Let me encourage you to respond in some way to at least one of these questions. You may be surprised by the freshness it brings to your lovemaking.

### *She Is Uninhibited*

The dictionary defines inhibition as "the act of holding back." We all have inhibitions we need to overcome. Inhibitions, inasmuch as they apply to sexual intimacy with your husband, can be more biblically described as pride, fear, or timidity. I think God's will for our sexual experience is expressed early in Scripture: "The man and his wife were both naked, and they felt no shame" (Genesis 2:25, NIV). After Adam and Eve sinned, they suddenly became ashamed and covered themselves with fig leaves. But in Christ we can again love each other without shame, totally free to give ourselves and enjoy ourselves to the fullest.

What holds you back from fully enjoying sexual intimacy? Ask God to search your heart and bring to light any reluctance and the roots of that reluctance. Only after you've discerned what these are, especially if the Bible calls them sin, can you begin to overcome them with a biblical mind-set and biblical actions.

For example, many women worry about what they consider to be physical imperfections. They feel too thin or too fat, too tall or too short, too dark or too light, and so on. But a biblical mind-set assures us we are created in the very image of God. Here's the clear message he gives us in his Word: "I have created you in my image. I make no mistakes. You are fearfully and wonderfully made" (see Genesis 1:27; Psalm 139:14). Do you believe this? You must! Stop comparing your body to the world's image of the perfect body. (What right does Hollywood have to determine physical perfection anyway?) Instead, find security in the truth that you are uniquely, fearfully, and wonderfully made! Your husband chose *you*, not anyone else. As you revel in that fact and freely give yourself to him, what may seem like physical imperfections to you will fade as you enjoy the unique way each of you is made.

I do want to encourage you to take care of the body God has given you. Attending to your physical needs—which might involve losing weight, gaining weight, exercising, or modifying your diet—is a wonderful way to improve your health and express love and respect for your husband. In addition, I've found that by taking care of myself as faithfully (not perfectly) as I can, then with a clear conscience I can focus on my husband and not myself. I can ask God's blessing and deepen my enjoyment in lovemaking.

### *She Is Aggressive*

Most husbands realize there is a lot more to sex than getting their biological cravings met by a passive wife. When we are warm and affectionate and aggressive, our men will feel loved and desired, not just endured.

Your husband may think about physical intimacy more than you do, but it's not his responsibility to initiate every instance of lovemaking. Look for opportunities to surprise him with an unexpected encounter or a creative approach. You may unlock a greater thrill for yourself as well!

## RESOLVING TO SEEK GOD'S BEST TOGETHER

Much of what Betsy and I have included in this chapter has been, of necessity, very basic. Space does not permit us to address the more complicated difficulties that may arise in a sexual relationship. Some sexual problems are addressed in our Recommended Reading list at the back of this book. As you talk openly with one another, get counsel, and benefit from additional resources, we're confident that God can bring you to the place where you can joyfully declare to each other, "You have stolen my heart . . . how delightful is your love . . . how much more pleasing is your love than wine" (Song 4:9-10, NIV).

In our marriage we have been working on a number of the areas covered in this chapter for many years. The knowledge that we will be growing in oneness and holiness throughout our marriage helps us not to become weary or discouraged. On the contrary, this biblical view allows us to press forward in faith, grateful for whatever progress we have been granted and hopeful for more.

In our experience God usually points to just one area at a time. But he does expect change, and he will always be giving us the grace and opportunity to mature. Thus he calls every couple to commit themselves to the process of repentance, growth, and change. So ask the Lord, "In what area must I improve? Where do I need to grow in order to serve my spouse more effectively in our sexual relationship?" Then take a few moments to listen.

God is eager to counsel or graciously convict as needed. If God is showing you that you've been pursuing your own sexual gratification without regard to your wife's needs, you need to repent and ask her forgiveness as well as God's. If your distaste for sex has caused you to deprive your husband, repent and seek God's help as you commit yourself to being available. Pray for your spouse and for your sexual relationship. If you've settled for second best, resolve now in your heart that you will pursue God's ultimate intent—thrilling sexual pleasure and intimacy in marriage. By God's grace, this can be one of the most exciting aspects of a love that lasts.

Just a few more pages and you will have finished this book. We want to thank and commend you for the time and effort you have invested, but we're not quite done! There are still some things we'd like to share about God's glorious gift of marriage.

So let's move into the Epilogue together!

# *An Epilogue:*
# WE'RE ALL JUST GETTING STARTED

Finally, here we are, so very close to the conclusion of our travels with you through your marriage journey. And what an excursion it has been! We've covered a lot of ground together and surveyed a lot of scenery.

But Betsy and I are also aware that so much more could be said about all that goes into the lifelong adventure called marriage. It was never our intention to write "the last word" on the subject. Nor do we believe we have touched on all the many topics or seasons that may very well have been a part of your marriage experience—seasons like adjusting to the first child, or topics like honoring your in-laws, or seasons when you have faithfully honored your wedding vows through financial difficulties, the inability to conceive children, or the grief of suffering or divorce. We are particularly humbled by those of you who, with full devotion, loved and honored your spouse even when your experience has included "till death do us part." We know that for many of you seasons like these are quite real.

And while we would never presume to say we understand every marriage, we do hope our efforts have pointed you to the One who does.

We hope and pray also that some of what we've shared will undergird, support, encourage, and direct you along the rest of your journey, wherever you might be right now. The Recommended Reading list is also designed to put you in touch with some of the wisdom, guidance, grace, and care that God has poured out through gifted leaders and authors. We are pleased to introduce you to them if you've never met before.

So as we draw to a close, thanks for letting us take this part of the trip with you. But, friends, it's not time to get out of the car. This is only the beginning of the trip!

If you recall back in Chapter One, we mentioned "The Ricuccis' Wild West Adventure." That's right, in 2002 Betsy and I made the memory of a lifetime with our four children. We drove 8,100 miles cross-country and back . . . in a Pontiac Montana minivan . . . in just three weeks! From Gaithersburg, Maryland, we drove straight through to St. Louis, Missouri, then straight through to Denver, Colorado. We drove to Mt. Rushmore in South Dakota, then to Cody, Wyoming, to Yellowstone National Park, and into the Grand Tetons. We headed to California to take in Yosemite and then drove down the California coast. From a little town named Cambria we headed east and took in the Grand Canyon. After a few more motels we arrived at my alma mater, Carson-Newman College in east Tennessee, and made our last stop (where else?) in Williamsburg, Virginia. There we visited Colonial America and a Busch Gardens theme park to celebrate our son Garrett's sixteenth birthday.

And yes, along the way we actually did stop to talk, gaze, marvel, take pictures (lots of pictures!), hike, explore, sleep in motels, share meals, and thoroughly enjoy the gift of being together as a family. We savored each and every leg of the trip and each and every destination. And we would do it all again in a minute if we could (well, maybe taking *four* weeks). You just have to try it sometime!

The planning was thrilling. We looked at maps, prepared an itinerary, made reservations, got recommendations from friends, and limited luggage to one bag each—mandatory. We were given a new digital camera so we could record our memories and share them when we got home. But as exciting as the reading, reviewing, shopping, and planning were, none of these were the journey and the adventure. Nothing could substitute for the actual trip—enjoying time together and God's creation.

We had to get in the car, trust and follow the maps, and start moving. And you know what? Through God's grace, wisdom, protection, and provision, we did it!

We saw vast plains, magnificent forests, picturesque lakes, rolling hills, majestic mountains, incredible canyons, rushing rivers, soaring geysers, star-drenched skies, spectacular sunsets, dramatic lightning storms, a searing desert, and the grand Pacific Ocean. We encountered and photographed moose, buffalo, elk, deer (which the kids kept reminding me we could see at home), and a bear (ask Betsy about it)! Many portions of the trip were breathtaking, awe-inspiring, and exhilarating. Some parts were just tedious and monotonous. Some of the hikes were pretty easy and peaceful, and some demanded extreme caution and stamina. Very often we didn't know what we would encounter until we got there. But that didn't matter. We wanted to take in everything we could. We believed God had blessed us with the opportunity for a memorable family adventure, and we were excited to take the journey, all of it, trusting God to give us grace to finish well.

Come to think of it, we feel the same way about our marriage . . . and yours!

That's why we wrote this book—to be sort of a combination map, compass, and trail guide. It's designed to help you explore and savor every step of your marriage journey. It is also intended to help you set a new and true direction from wherever you are right now. We hope and pray that this book will help you handle effectively much of what you will encounter along the way.

But again, even this little volume isn't the journey. Reading a book is not taking the entire trip. Regardless of how many miles you've already traveled, so much of the glorious adventure of marriage is still before you. Whether you are enjoying open road and clear skies, or whether you are struggling up yet another mountain in stormy weather . . . whether you are just pulling out of your driveway or nearly to the end of the trip home . . . God is there with you to help you finish the journey, and finish it well.

We have covered many topics in our time together, but we'd like to close with a few "packing and travel tips" for the rest of your own marriage adventure.

First of all, don't begin any leg of the journey with a focus on all that *you* have to do! Concerns like that are probably motivated by self-sufficient pride. Begin with what God has done for you in Jesus Christ. That's humility and faith. The gospel redeems the past, provides for the present, and prepares for the future. In marriage, it is God's activity through the finished work of Christ, applied in our lives by the indwelling Holy Spirit, that encourages and enables us and ensures our future. Every journey must begin here.

Study and know the Word of God. It is God's lamp for your feet and a light for your path (Psalm 119:105); his water for washing, purifying, and refreshing your soul (Ephesians 5:26-27); his compass for discerning the direction of your heart (Hebrews 4:12); and his field guide, if you will . . . perfect, authoritative, accurate, and powerful to equip and take you each step of the way (2 Timothy 3:16-17). Be a humble learner. Grace will always follow.

And finally, don't travel through marriage alone. Don't travel isolated from one another, or isolated as a couple from the local church. Being alone wasn't good in the garden (Genesis 2:18), and it isn't a wise way to take a journey today (Proverbs 15:22). Being alone separates you from God's means of growth and blessing (Proverbs 18:1; Romans 12:5; 1 Corinthians 12:18-21; Ephesians 4:15-16). And failing to meet with other believers is a bad and dangerous habit that leaves you vulnerable (Hebrews 10:24-25). Jesus is building his church, not isolated wilderness wanderers. God wants your journey to be shared.

Well, friends, it looks like you're all packed and ready to head out on the rest of your adventure. Just one more thing before you set off. Please prayerfully reread Chapter One of this book. Then pray each day about some part of the trip. Let the Lord fill you with faith and vision for a marvelous adventure on the magnificent journey called marriage! And later, when you're near the end of the journey and discover you're close to going home, pause and thank God for all the ways he met you, blessed you, and made yours a love that lasts!

## THE BEGINNING

# Questions for Discussion, Evaluation, and Application

Thank you so much for your desire to bring greater glory to God through your marriage by applying what you have read in this book! The following questions can be used effectively by an individual couple, in a local-church counseling ministry, or in small-group settings with other couples. Whatever the context, we recommend that you:

• Talk in an atmosphere of relaxation and privacy.

• Begin with prayer. Ask God to grant you illumination by his Holy Spirit for the purpose of personal responsibility and conviction and practical application.

• Consider addressing just a question or two at any one time. This will allow thought and discussion to be more thorough and your goals to be more realistic.

• Take notes to follow up on your thoughts, questions, and plan of action.

• If the discussions so far have involved just you and your spouse, take time to share your discussion with another couple in your church.

## CHAPTER 1
## THE JOURNEY OF A LIFETIME: WHERE IT ALL BEGINS

1. Until now, what have been your primary sources of instruction and example for marriage? Have these influences been biblically accurate? Please explain.

2. How has this chapter altered your perspective about the purpose for your marriage? Which specific aspects of your lives and relationship need to be more God-centered? What steps can you take to begin that process?

3. Where specifically does the Word of God need to have more influence in your marriage? Which verses or passages of Scripture need to be applied? What would change look like in those areas?

4. What is the gospel? Does your current understanding of the gospel differ from the understanding you held prior to reading this chapter? If so, how?

5. Using the list of truths about the gospel appearing in this chapter, how can you more specifically apply God's grace and the gospel to your engagement or marriage? Where do you see areas of weakness in your life or relationship that reveal a deficient application of the gospel?

6. What role does the local church currently play in the development and growth of your marriage? If the role is currently minimal, what must you do to apply the Scriptures cited in this chapter about the church? Who are the close friends with whom you can discuss any detail of your life or marriage?

7. What part of this chapter has had the greatest impact on you? Where did you receive the greatest encouragement? What is one step of obedience or application that God is calling you to take as a couple? With whom will you begin to discuss this?

8. What is one thing from this chapter you would like to see your betrothed or spouse apply more consistently? How can you encourage, support, or help him or her in that process?

### *For Further Study*

Saying, "This mystery is profound" (Ephesians 5:32), Paul compares marriage to the relationship between Christ and the church. To better understand this mystery, examine these verses: Isaiah 54:5-8; Jeremiah 2:2; 31:1-6; Hosea 2:19-20; Revelation 19:7; 21:2.

## CHAPTER 2
## LEADING WITH LOVE: THE ROLE OF THE HUSBAND

1. How does understanding the role relationships in the Trinity, in combination with the story of creation, help you understand male and female, leadership and supportive submission? Has your understanding of roles changed since reading this chapter? How so?

2. Do you as a couple agree with the terms *headship*, *leadership*, *submission*, and *subordination* as they relate to your roles in marriage? If you disagree with one another in your understanding of these terms, how will you resolve those differences?

3. Men, why is a clear understanding of the gospel vital to fulfilling your role as a husband? What are specific ways this can make a difference in your marriage?

4. How can you begin to love your wife more graciously, sacrificially, and redemptively?

5. What does it mean to live with your wife or fiancée in an understanding way—say, when she disagrees with you? When she is tempted with anxiety or fear? When she is sinning in her words, behavior, or attitudes?

6. How would you evaluate your practice of honoring your wife or fiancée? Would she agree? Give specific examples of ways you have honored her. Why is honoring your wife more a matter of your heart than of her performance?

7. Ask your wife or fiancée if any person, activity, or possession, at any time, seems more important to you than her.

8. How would your wife or fiancée evaluate your leadership, decision-making, and exercise of authority in your relationship? Is it humble? Consistent? Timely? Is it motivated by a desire for God's glory and her good? Ask her for examples.

9. Do you demonstrate godly and loving leadership by helping her to identify and overcome patterns of sin in her life? Give an illustration of how you have done this. What might explain any deficiency in this expression of love? In what specific ways can you improve?

10. Do you lead your wife or fiancée by example in your pursuit of God and personal godliness?

11. Does any aspect of your leadership make it difficult for your wife or fiancée to submit to and follow you?

### *For Further Study*

Meditate on Ephesians 5:25-27. What are some further expressions of Christ's love for his Bride? Genuine love includes helping our wives overcome sin and grow in godliness. How can you demonstrate this form of love in your marriage?

## Chapter 3
## Walking in Wisdom: The Role of the Wife

1. Before reading this chapter, what came to mind when you thought of the role of the wife? Has your perspective changed? If so, how? What made the difference?

2. How does your understanding of Proverbs 14:1 encourage you as you consider all the details and activities that go into being a wife, mother, and keeper of your home?

3. Based on what you have read in this chapter, how would you explain the meaning of being called to be a "helper" to your husband?

4. As you review the expressions of love listed in this chapter, where do you already see God's grace in helping you apply them? In what ways can you improve?

5. In what specific ways can you demonstrate sincere respect for your husband? What might explain any deficiencies in these areas up until now?

6. How does understanding the role relationships in the Trinity, in combination with the story of creation, help your understanding of the leadership of a husband and the supportive submission of a wife?

7. Ask your husband or fiancé to share the ways in which you demonstrate biblical submission in your relationship. In what ways can you improve?

8. How would you summarize the encouragement and opportunities a wife can find in Proverbs 31?

9. Explain the position of influence a wife holds in a marriage. How have you influenced your husband? How would you like to influence him in the future?

### *For Further Study*

Meditate on Genesis 3:1-13, 16. What effect do you believe this series of events has had on the way men and women relate today?

## CHAPTER 4
## RELATIONAL INTIMACY: THE GOAL OF OUR COMMUNICATION

1. What does Genesis 2:18-24 tell you about God's assessment of isolation and his intention for the relationship between a husband and wife?

2. What does honesty in communication look like? Are there areas of your lives and relationship that you find difficult to talk about? What steps will you take to bring those areas into the light of fellowship and communication?

3. As you evaluate the communication between you, where do you see areas of pride in your life? In what ways can you more consistently demonstrate and practice humility?

4. What practices can you consistently include in your communication and fellowship with one another that would demonstrate your desire to change and grow in godliness?

5. What subjects do you two talk about most consistently? Most enthusiastically? Most confidently? What do these topics, and the way you talk about them, reveal about your passions and priorities?

6. How can you begin to develop a more vigorous lifestyle of spiritual discourse? What might explain any deficiencies in this area?

7. Describe your current practice of the spiritual disciplines in terms of consistency and content. To what extent does your fellowship with God make its way into your daily conversations with one another? What can you do to enrich the spiritual content of those conversations?

8. Compare your communication with one another now and when you were first married. What have you read in this chapter that gives you hope and anticipation for deeper communication and richer relational intimacy?

### *For Further Study*

Read Ephesians 5:18b-20. Which topics and practices described in this passage can you begin to include in your conversations? Which topics, if any, do you currently practice, but not always in ways that are helpful?

## Chapter 5
## Grace to Those Who Hear: The Content of Our Communication

1. Describe how you differ *from* one another in your patterns of communication *with* one another. How do you typically respond to those differences? How do those differences affect your communication and fellowship?

2. Discuss and evaluate the extent to which you are comfortable with and consistently use all the listed "varieties of talk." Do you seem to major on one or two types, employing other types only infrequently? Are you typically in agreement about and satisfied with the types of communication you choose? Are you satisfied that you usually choose the type that fits the occasion? If not, why not?

3. Are either of you reluctant to engage in consistent communication and fellowship with one another? Do any of the excuses listed in the "Time to Talk" section hinder your initiative or participation in conversation?

4. Evaluate your practice of both planned and spontaneous communication and fellowship. Would you say your communication is consistent or sporadic? Do you believe you are current with one another on the matters of greatest importance? Give examples.

5. What are the greatest challenges you face in pursuing consistent and fruitful communication with one another? What needs to change internally and externally in order for this to happen? If you are an engaged couple, do you think your communication will be different after the wedding? How so?

6. To what extent is encouragement a prominent element in your communication with one another? Are you frequently giving glory to God for his activity and grace in your lives? Where can this improve? What might explain any deficiencies in this area?

7. Is consistent, clear, grace-filled correction a regular part of your communication? Do you see correction as an expression of your love for one another? If this is a weak area, what attitude in your heart might explain the weakness?

8. Are you faithful to confess your sin to others and invite their correction? Do you do so as an expression of your awareness of your need to grow, and your need for others to help you grow? What might an absence of initiative in these areas reveal about your heart?

9. What is the next step you can take to develop and improve your communication and fellowship with one another? What change, by God's grace, do you look forward to in your relationship as a result of this step?

### *For Further Study*

What two types of people are mentioned in Proverbs 9:8? Describe each. As you read David's appeal in Psalm 141:5, which type of person does he appear to be? Which type are you?

## CHAPTER 6
## THE HEART OF CONFLICT: RESTORING COMMUNICATION

1. Describe a past conflict between you that you now look back on with amusement or even laughter. Having read this chapter, how would you now handle such a situation differently?

2. Consider again the gospel. How does the gospel influence your thinking about your own sin and any sin committed against you? How can considering and applying the gospel make a difference in a conflict?

3. Think of the many ways you and your spouse are different from one another. Make a list. Then jot down the matters or topics about which you simply disagree or have differing opinions. How do you typically respond to those differences? Do you accept and appreciate one another's non-sinful differences? Do you criticize and contend?

4. Describe a recent or memorable conflict between you. Now read James 4:1-4. How do these verses and the pattern of conflict mentioned in this chapter apply here? Go step by step from *Desire* to *Destruction.*

Knowing what you know now, how would the conversation be different if the desire was again met with disappointment?

5. Describe a conflict between you that was resolved biblically. In what ways have you and your spouse benefited from that experience?

6. Evaluate your practice of confessing sin to one another—consistently, sincerely, and specifically, in biblical terms, and without qualification.

7. Evaluate your practice of extending forgiveness to one another—consistently, sincerely, and specifically, in biblical terms, and without qualification.

8. Do any conflicts remain unresolved between you? What couples in your church can you go to for counsel and care on this or any other matter?

### *For Further Study*

Meditate on Matthew 7:1-5. Read through each verse slowly and carefully. What would your last conflict have looked like had you applied these verses in detail? Does this give you hope for your next conflict?

### *A Suggested Plan for Fruitful Conflict Resolution*

1. Prepare a list of Scriptures on the topics of pleasing God, anger, pride, speech, love, etc.

2. When trying to resolve a conflict, at the first sign of fresh temptation or sin, stop and pray.

3. If the temptation increases or sin continues, pause the conflict-resolution conversation.

4. Find separate, quiet places to be alone with God.

5. Begin to go over your list of Scriptures, asking God to convict you.

6. Pray and confess sin where God has revealed a "log" in your eye or a craving in your heart.

7. Confess that sin to God, and ask for grace and godly sorrow that will lead to repentance.

8. Reconvene after fifteen to twenty minutes.

9. Sit down together with your Bibles open.

10. Pray, asking God to guide and control your hearts and conversation.

11. Confess all cravings and "logs" for which God has convicted you regarding the temptation or sin that put your conversation on pause.

12. Ask specific forgiveness as necessary.

13. Extend complete forgiveness as necessary.

14. Resume the initial conversation, seeking to resolve the initial conflict.

### CHAPTER 7
### IT NEVER HAS TO GET OLD: THE SOUL OF ROMANCE

1. Take a few moments for each of you to write out your own description of romance. Then compare your descriptions. How are they similar? How are they different? Any surprises? How do you both respond to those differences?

2. How does your current pursuit and practice of romance compare with your experience during your engagement and first year of marriage? What is different and why? If romance has diminished, what have you grown to desire or love more?

3. As you consider some of the expressions of passion and romance found in the Song of Songs, in which areas are you consistent? In which areas do you need to improve? What needs to change in your heart as well as in your behavior?

4. Review the list of possible "little foxes" that can rob a marriage of passion, romance, and intimacy. Are you able to identify the sin in your heart that has allowed any of these to persist? What specific step of repentance can you take to begin to rid your garden of at least one of these predators?

5. The outward practice of romance begins with an inward passion. Take some time alone to consider God's goodness and wisdom in giving you your spouse. What do you love, appreciate, respect, and admire in him or her? Write out your thoughts in detail. How can you begin to creatively communicate those thoughts and feelings to your spouse?

6. As you prioritize romance as a way of life, which practices do you most look forward to pursuing? For which idea or activity might you

need help in creativity, planning, or follow-through? What part of your week can you set aside to allow for the regular planning of romantic ways to express love for your spouse?

7. Describe (as appropriate for the context) some of your most memorable experiences of romance. What made them particularly meaningful?

### *For Further Study*

Desire and affection are to be an integral part of the marriage relationship (see Genesis 29:20; Song of Songs 7:10). If your desire is deficient, what needs to change in your heart? Then what needs to change in your action?

## Chapter 8
## Just the Two of You: The Wonder of Sexual Intimacy

For group discussion, these questions should be considered by men and women in separate groups. Please share honestly, but remember to share in a way that honors your spouse.

### *Men:*

1. What were the primary sources of influence, example, and instruction that formed your initial understanding of sexuality? Were they biblical? If not, in what ways were these influences different from that of Scripture?

2. In your own words, what is God's plan and promise for sexual intimacy in the context of marriage? What is your basis for this understanding?

3. What is God's will and warning regarding the neglect or withholding of sexual intimacy?

4. Are there any fears, concerns, or reservations that you carry regarding any aspect of sexual intimacy in your marriage? Please explain. What is the basis for these concerns?

5. Evaluate your pursuit of help and counsel from others to improve your sexual relationship with your wife. Begin with the extent to which you ask her in humility to evaluate that aspect of your marriage.

6. In addition to your wife, to whom do you or will you speak about any questions, concerns, or the overall health of your sexual relationship in your marriage?

7. Ask for your wife's evaluation of your sexual relationship, starting with these areas:

a. Frequency with which you initiate conversations expressing interest and concern about her sexual enjoyment, pleasure, and satisfaction.

b. Frequency of your initiative in lovemaking.

c. Your cultivation of relational and emotional intimacy preceding your sexual initiative.

d. Your skill at creating the proper mood, whether lovemaking is planned or spontaneous.

e. Your leadership in continuing to develop a richer and more satisfying sexual relationship for you both.

8. What specific steps can you begin to take (both in your heart and in application) to develop a more intimate, pleasurable, and satisfying sexual relationship with your wife?

*Women:*

1. What were the primary sources of influence, example, and instruction that formed your initial understanding of sexuality? Were they biblical? If not, in what ways were these influences different from that of Scripture?

2. In your own words, what is God's plan and promise for sexual intimacy in the context of marriage? What is your basis for this understanding?

3. What is God's will and warning regarding the neglect or withholding of sexual intimacy?

4. Are there any fears, concerns, or reservations that you carry regarding any aspect of sexual intimacy in your marriage? Please explain. What is the basis for these concerns?

5. Evaluate your pursuit of help and counsel from others to improve your sexual relationship with your husband. Begin with the extent to which you ask him in humility to evaluate that aspect of your marriage.

6. In addition to your husband, to whom do you or will you speak

about any questions, concerns, or the overall health of your sexual relationship in your marriage?

7. Ask for your husband's evaluation of your sexual relationship, starting with these areas:

a. Frequency with which you initiate conversations expressing interest and concern about his sexual enjoyment, pleasure, and satisfaction.

b. Your responsiveness to his initiative in lovemaking.

c. Your cultivation of relational and emotional intimacy preceding sexual initiative.

d. Your skill at helping to create the proper mood, whether lovemaking is planned or spontaneous.

e. Your receptivity, responsiveness, and initiative in continuing to develop a richer and more satisfying sexual relationship for you both.

8. What specific steps can you begin to take (both in your heart and in application) to develop a more intimate, pleasurable, and satisfying sexual relationship with your husband?

### *For Further Study*

Read Song of Songs 5:2-6. Do you and your spouse talk humbly and honestly about your desires, disappointments, and delights in your lovemaking experience? Are there things you need to share about one or more previous experiences together, in preparation for the next time you make love?

# Recommended Reading by Topic


### CHURCH

Joshua Harris, *Stop Dating the Church* (Sisters, OR: Multnomah, 2004).

### COMMUNICATION AND CONFLICT RESOLUTION

Ken Sande, *The Peacemaker* (Grand Rapids, MI: Baker, 1997).

Paul Tripp, *War of Words* (Phillipsburg, NJ: P & R, 2000).

### COURTSHIP

Joshua Harris, *Boy Meets Girl* (Sisters, OR: Multnomah, 2005).

### DIVORCE

Jay Adams, *Marriage, Divorce and Remarriage in the Bible* (Grand Rapids, MI: Zondervan, 1986).

John Murray, *Divorce* (Phillipsburg, NJ: P & R, 1987).

### DOCTRINE

Wayne Grudem, *Bible Doctrine* (Grand Rapids, MI: Zondervan, 1999).

J. I. Packer, *Knowing God* (Downers Grove, IL: InterVarsity Press, 1993).

### THE GOSPEL

C.J. Mahaney, *Living the Cross-Centered Life* (Sisters, OR: Multnomah, 2002).

### MASCULINITY AND FEMININITY

Wayne Grudem, *Evangelical Feminism and Biblical Truth* (Sisters, OR: Multnomah, 2004).

Wayne Grudem and John Piper, editors, *Recovering Biblical Manhood and Womanhood* (Wheaton, IL: Crossway Books, 1991).

John Piper, *What's the Difference?* (Wheaton, IL: Crossway Books, 2001).

### MEN

Joshua Harris, *Sex Is Not the Problem (Lust Is)* (Sisters, OR: Multnomah, 2005).

C.J. Mahaney, *Sex, Romance, and the Glory of God* (Wheaton, IL: Crossway Books, 2004).

### SANCTIFICATION

C.J. Mahaney, *Humility: True Greatness* (Sisters, OR: Multnomah, 2005).

Paul Tripp, *Instruments in the Redeemer's Hands* (Phillipsburg, NJ: P & R, 2002).

Thomas Watson, *The Doctrine of Repentance* (Carlisle, PA: Banner of Truth, 1999).

### SEXUAL INTIMACY

Ed and Gaye Wheat, *Intended for Pleasure* (Grand Rapids, MI: Revell, 1997).

### SPIRITUAL DISCIPLINES

John Piper, *When I Don't Desire God: How to Fight for Joy* (Wheaton, IL: Crossway Books, 2004).

Donald Whitney, *Spiritual Disciplines for the Christian Life* (Colorado Springs: NavPress, 1994).

### SUFFERING

Jerry Bridges, *Trusting God* (Colorado Springs: NavPress, 1991).

Don Carson, *How Long, O Lord?* (Grand Rapids, MI: Baker, 1991).

Charles Spurgeon, *Beside Still Waters* (Nashville: Thomas Nelson, 1999).

### WOMEN

Carolyn Mahaney, *Feminine Appeal* (Wheaton, IL: Crossway Books, 2004).

# Notes


1. Jerry Bridges, *The Discipline of Grace* (Colorado Springs: NavPress, 1994), p. 17.
2. Joshua Harris, *Stop Dating the Church: Fall in Love with the Family of God* (Sisters, OR: Multnomah, 2004), p. 50.
3. John Piper, in *Recovering Biblical Manhood and Womanhood*, Wayne Grudem and John Piper, general editors (Wheaton, IL: Crossway Books, 1991), p. 35.
4. Ibid., p. 36.
5. Ibid., p. 38.
6. Ibid., p. 39.
7. Ibid., p. 40.
8. Paul David Tripp, *Instruments in the Redeemer's Hands* (Phillipsburg, NJ: P&R, 2002), p. 15.
9. Carolyn Mahaney, *Feminine Appeal* (Wheaton, IL: Crossway Books, 2004), p. 37.
10. Charles Spurgeon, *Morning & Evening*, Morning, February 19.
11. George MacDonald, *An Anthology*, ed. C. S. Lewis (New York: Macmillan, 1978), in George MacDonald, *Unspoken Sermons* (Whitefish, MT: Kessinger Publishing, 2004), p. 75.
12. Carolyn Mahaney, *Feminine Appeal*, p. 142.
13. John Piper, in *Recovering Biblical Manhood and Womanhood*, p. 53.
14. John Piper, "A Woman Who Fears the Lord Is to be Praised," a sermon delivered May 10, 1981; http://www.desiringgod.org/library/sermons/81/051081.html
15. Derek Kidner, *The Proverbs: An Introduction and Commentary* (Downers Grove, IL: InterVarsity Press, 1964), p. 50.

16. Ibid., p. 184.

17. Charles Bridges, *A Commentary on Proverbs* (Carlisle, PA: Banner of Truth, 1994), p. 133.

18. J. I. Packer, *God's Words* (Grand Rapids, MI: Baker, 1992), p. 196.

19. Paul Tripp, "Speaking Redemptively," *Journal of Biblical Counseling*, Vol. 16, No. 3 (Spring 1998), p. 18.

20. John Owen, *The Works of John Owen*, Volume VI, *Temptation and Sin* (Carlisle, PA: Banner of Truth, 1967), p. 20.

21. Paul David Tripp and Timothy Lane, *Helping Others Change* (Winston-Salem, NC: Punch Press, 2005), p. 8.

22. Spurgeon, *Morning & Evening*, Evening, April 7.

23. Thomas Watson, *The Doctrine of Repentance* (Carlisle, PA: Banner of Truth, 1999), pp. 29-30.

24. Ken Sande, *The Peacemaker*, second edition (Grand Rapids, MI: Baker, 1997), pp. 188-189.

25. Ibid., p. 26.

26. C.J. Mahaney, *Sex, Romance, and the Glory of God: What Every Christian Husband Needs to Know* (Wheaton, IL: Crossway Books, 2004), p. 63.

27. Ibid., p. 86.

28. Ed Wheat and Gaye Wheat, *Intended for Pleasure* (Grand Rapids, MI: Revell, 1977), p. 79.

29. Ibid., p. 81.

30. C.J. Mahaney, *Sex, Romance, and the Glory of God*, p. 28.

31. Carolyn Mahaney, *Feminine Appeal*, p. 84.

## THE Ricuccis

### *Also Highly Recommend* THESE *Resources*

***Worship God Live* (Sovereign Grace Music)**
This CD was recorded live at our home church, Covenant Life, and contains 14 songs; each one rich in the glorious gospel and grace of our Lord Jesus Christ. Because the cross-centered worship here is so like what we experience each Sunday, this CD has become one of our all-time favorites. When you hear the truth of Scripture and behold the glory of God displayed in these songs, you won't just listen...you'll want to worship.

***Sex, Romance, and the Glory of God: What Every Christian Husband Needs to Know***
C.J. Mahaney (Crossway)
The title says it all. Husbands, this book is a "must read." (And wives, there's a chapter at the end just for you.) Through C.J.'s inimitable blend of uncompromising truth, practical and accessible application, and distinctive humor, this book teaches a husband how to cultivate the kind of thorough, biblical intimacy and passion with his wife that God intends for you both to enjoy...not only as a wonderful event, but as a way of life!

***Feminine Appeal: Seven Virtues of a Godly Wife and Mother***
Carolyn Mahaney (Crossway)
In a way that is exceptionally winsome and graciously bold, Carolyn presents the power, wisdom, and timeless relevance of Titus 2. Women of all ages will benefit from her clear teaching, compelling example, and model of biblical instruction.

***To Teach What Is Good: Wisdom for Women from Titus 2***
Carolyn Mahaney (Sovereign Grace Ministries)
This is the audio series on which *Feminine Appeal* is based. It's a great introduction not only to this passage of Scripture, but to Carolyn, her considerable teaching gift, and her heart for the women of this and future generations. Available as an eight-message CD set, one complete MP3 CD, or as individual MP3 downloads.

***According to Plan***
C.J. and Carolyn Mahaney (Sovereign Grace Ministries)
These three messages formed a seminar of the same name. In it, the Mahaneys provide a biblical understanding of God's purpose for marriage, a husband's responsibilities, and biblical submission. This series really will help you to establish and enjoy a marriage that is built according to God's plan. Available on a complete MP3 CD or as individual MP3 downloads.

Find it all online at the Sovereign Grace Store (www.sovereigngracestore.com)
**www.SovereignGraceMinistries.org**